Jasmin Akash M.A.

HOLOGRAPHIC MEDITATION
The Twelve Elixirs of Life

HOLOGRAPHIC MEDITATION
The Twelve Elixirs of Life

ISBN: 978-0-9905455-0-7

Copyright © 2001 by Jasmin Akash. All rights reserved.

Holographic Meditation Institute, 511 Kupulau Dr., Kihei, Hawaii, 96753
Publisher: Petar Todorovic, Vladislav Todorovic
Editor: Neil Gillespie
Design by Jev®a & ::Meda
Photography: Milorad Popovic
Prepress: Foto Dunav, R. Mirkovica 6, Smederevo, YU
Printing: Foto Dunav

No part of this book may be used or reproduced or transmitted in any form or by any means, except for the quotation of brief passages in a review, without written permission by the publisher.

CIP - Katalogizacija u publikaciji
Narodna biblioteka Srbije, Beograd
133.2
AKASH, Jasmin
Holographic Meditation: The Twelve
Elixirs of Life / Jasmin Akash; [photography
Milorad Popovic]. - Beograd: P. Todorovic :
V. Todorovic, 2001 (Beograd: Foto Dunav) . -
165 str. : ilustr. :20 cm
Slika autora. - Tiraz 500. - Bibliografija:
str. 157-163.
159.98
a) Meditacija b) Psihotehnika
ID=90607116

Originally published in 2001.
Second Printing 2015 by
Akash Khi Publishing
Kihei, Hawaii, USA

For more information, please contact Jasmin Akash:
info@akashkhi.com   www.akashkhi.com

Contents

Introduction

Philosophy of Oneness

I The Flesh of God
        The Quest for Primordial Oneness 7
        Strangers or Relatives? 10
        Recycled Stardust 11
        Phantoms of Light 13
        Pixelate, Blend, Emboss! 15
        Why Spoil the Fun? 17
        The Separation Syndrome 18

The Path

I Our True Nature
      Yin and Yang of Creation 27
      Windows into Transcendence 29
      The Mind's Eye 30
      Unified Awareness .32
      The Art of Hologazing 35
      Wave Nature Meditation 36
      Holographic Nature Meditation 39
      Complementary Nature Meditation 41
      Visual Koans 43

II Happiness
      Indra's Net of Pearls 49
      The Twelvefold Path 51
      The Triads 55
      The Earth Mirrors the Sky 59
      Corona 61

III If The Hands Could Talk
      Ancient Mudras and Yantras 67
      Virtual Holo-Symbol 70
      Alchemy of the Hands 72
      The Common Ground 75
      Taming the Monkey Mind 77
      Shaking the Tree of Knowledge 80
      Reaping the Fruits .81
      Prototype Meditation Sequence 82

The Twelve Elixirs

I How Do I Think?
    Spirit 90
    Matter 94
    Oneness 100

II How Do I Act?
    Compassion 106
    Non-harming 110
    Love 114

III How Do I Feel?
    Power 120
    Freedom 126
    Wholeness 132

IV How Do I Materialize?
    Prosperity 140
    Self-mastery 144
    Self-actualization 148

Notes
Bibliography

Introduction

Happiness is the essence of life. It represents the ultimate driving force behind our goals and desires, and we measure our every success and failure with this universal yardstick. Instead of happiness our lives are often filled with suffering, the opposite extreme. That compels us to seek the guiding light that can point us in the right direction, toward the achievement of happiness as the most precious possession. The puzzling complexity of existence often obscures the path to happiness in a veil of mystery.

Holographic Mudra Meditation is a contemporary philosophy whose primary goal is the elimination of suffering caused by ignorance of our true nature. In Part One, we diagnose the universal root of human suffering. In Part Two and Three, we learn mind-expanding 'holographic' mudra meditation techniques, called Hologazing, that serve as a catalyst for a rapid personal transformation, leading to wholeness and ultimately greater happiness in life.

The philosophy of Holographic Mudra Meditation is based on a new scientific theory of reality - *the holographic paradigm* - and universal spiritual principles. Reflecting the spirit of the new era, this modern technology is designed for people interested in self-improvement and spiritual growth in the context of our contemporary lifestyle and mentality. The ultimate goal is not transcendental aloofness, but bettering ourselves and our day-to-day existence. In that sense, Holographic Mudra Meditation has a practical, down-to-earth application and fundamentally supports who we are as human beings *today*.

Philosophy of Oneness

1. The Flesh of God

1. The Flesh of God

The Quest for Primordial Oneness

Looking into the past from our contemporary plateau, we witness an enormous spiritual heritage of our evolving humanity. Christianity, Islam, Buddhism, Hinduism and many other spiritual traditions are the pillars of wisdom, the supporting superstructure of the monumental library that narrates the story of more than 15 billion years of Creation.

For an individual seeker, such a wealth of knowledge and information opens up many sacred pages into the domain of Spirit. In the quest for happiness and Truth there are undoubtedly many paths that we can follow. They may lead to universities, churches or holy temples. We may seek guidance from esteemed teachers and scholars or at the feet of the gurus. At the same time the complexity of available information and the paradoxical diversity of spiritual traditions can be confusing. Comparing the differences and sorting out the many incongruities is time-consuming; it can slow us down or even discourage us from the path. Throughout history, blind adherence to the letter of the law often became a source of conflict and mutual destruction amongst the people of different spiritual orientations.

To avoid such obstacles, it is important to remember that all spiritual traditions are essentially different parcels of a basic truth which is eternal and universal. It is vital therefore that we abandon our rigid attachments to external forms and look instead for the common denominator. What ties diverse spiritual paths together? What is the commonly shared wisdom of their teachings?

The answer to all these questions is the Oneness of all creation.

In ancient times sages spoke of the absolute Oneness of life with an irrevocable sense of knowing and confidence, even though there was no scientific evidence available at that time to verify their insights. Thousands of years later, with scientific confirmation at hand, such profound accuracy of intuitive perception appears nothing less than miraculous. In fact, the concept of Oneness formed the foundations of the world's greatest religions. In Hinduism, the unifying reality of Oneness is called Brahman. Indian Rishis referred to it as the 'womb of all things' or 'the navel of the universe'.[1] The Buddhist uses the term Dharma-kaya, Body of Being, to express the same basic idea.[2] In the Chinese tradition we come across the concept of Tao and the Yin/Yang symbol.[3] In Western religions the principle of Oneness is conveyed through the exclusive adoration of one central deity: Yahweh, Allah, Christ.

Despite the differences between symbols and approaches, the highest ideal of all spiritual traditions is the same: to attain Oneness, a state characterized by the expansion of mental boundaries and a feeling of being united with the whole of Creation.

For most people the true meaning of Oneness is rather abstract and difficult to

1. The Flesh of God

translate into our down-to-earth daily life. In fact, our sensory perceptions are continually reassuring us that we are anything but united. What does the sun, light years away, have to do with frozen icebergs of the North Pole? What is the basis for 'sameness' between living beings and dead objects? Without an easily recognizable logic behind them, such paradoxical extremes are rather difficult to consider as a unified whole. The truth is that things are exactly the same even though they look different. Odd as it may seem, everything in the visible universe belongs in the same basket of undifferentiated primordial Oneness.

Grasping the true meaning of Oneness is obviously not an easy task. In fact we can never understand it fully without also understanding the totality of existence. In order to know why and how Oneness represents our true nature, we must reach behind the scene of Nature's mysterious factory of Life and uncover her secrets.

Thousands of years ago science as we know it today did not exist. It was the role of spiritual traditions to provide us with such answers which they fulfilled through extensive use of symbols and metaphoric narration. The encrypted language behind spiritual riddles, paradoxes and parables was considered the most appropriate tool for conveying the hidden meaning behind universal Truths. It was thought suitable because it stimulated the mind to make intuitive leaps toward higher knowledge, beyond the trappings of the intellect. At the same time, ordinary language was considered too limited to express the complexities of cosmic laws and spiritual experiences.

In the last 100 years, new physics has been able to provide us with fresh and revolutionary insights into the invisible layers of the material world. Subjugating matter to gigantic particle accelerators and bombing its atoms enabled scientists to lift the veil from the mystery of creation. As we shall see from the following pages Oneness of all creation is no longer just a spiritual enigma to be transmitted via esoteric symbology, but a scientific fact of life which coincides fundamentally with metaphysical speculations of the past.

Strangers or Relatives?

At first glance, judging by external characteristics, we appear to be radically different from other forms of life. There seems to be little in common between a human being, a grasshopper, a rose, a whale or an eagle. But looks can be deceptive. Scientific research today has provided us with proof that we are greatly more interconnected than meets the eye. In fact every person, every animal and plant, every visible and invisible life-form, stems from the same ancestral root which can be traced far back into the past, an estimated 3.8 billion years ago. Fossil deposits indicate that all living species are related to each other through a common ancestor - a tiny bacterium. This single-celled organism represents the original root of Oneness which continued to branch and re-branch, expanding into an impressive Tree of Life.[4] Today, there are more than 3 million different species inhabiting the Earth, with humans as the most evolved in a long chain of Life.

DNA is more proof that even the most different life forms are genetically related, sharing kindred molecular structures. DNA represents the genetic alphabet, providing necessary information for the assembly of the species. Although the information content varies from one species to another, the basic chemical structure of DNA is universal, built out of 4 organic molecules: adenine, thymine, guanine, and cytosine.[5] The letters A, T, G, and C which stand for those chemical elements are the only four letters of the DNA genetic code alphabet. It is miraculous how so many diverse living creatures came into existence through endless variations in the sequence of just four genetic letters. We owe our uniqueness as human beings solely to the modifications of this uni-

1. The Flesh of God

versally shared genetic material. We should therefore always keep in mind that all living creatures crossing our life path are 'cousins' from the same family tree.

Recycled Stardust

Seeing the Oneness of all organic life is one thing, but qualifying both organic and inorganic life as the same substance of living matter represents a stretch of our logical minds. Yet scientists are saying today that there is no sharp division between living and non-living things, just as there is no fundamental difference between the carbon atom in our body, in a diamond or in a piece of coal. According to Bohm's scientific theory of 'undivided wholeness', there is no fundamental difference between life, matter and consciousness. They are essentially different "projections of a common ground."[6]

External differences between rocks, plants, animals or any other created thing completely disappear at the subatomic level where the physical world reveals itself as a wavelike phenomenon, a web of energy frequencies and their interconnections. What we normally perceive through our senses as solid things with different qualities and textures are just an infinite variety of energy patterns which have become permanently interlocked. This fundamental interconnectedness of all subatomic processes is the primordial root of the Oneness of all life.

According to the science of cosmology, Oneness is something 'a priori', preceding all that has ever been created in the long process of evolution. We can trace it back about 15 billion years, when our universe was born in a scientifically speculated, cataclysmic burst of light called the Big Bang.[7] Prior to this titanic explosion the universe was in a state of cosmic Oneness, with no distinct features. What evolved into an estimated 10^{50} tons of matter[8] which the observable universe contains today was originally an infinitesimally concentrated pinpoint of energy. Out of this single seed Creation flowered into millions of distinctly shaped galaxies, stars and planets, spreading out into vast cosmic regions.

Matter was born within seconds of the Big Bang explosion, marked by the emergence of the first subatomic particles called quarks.[9] Through their joining together, an assembly of protons and neutrons began. Through combinations of protons and neutrons the first elements - hydrogen and helium - became manifest. Adding different combinations of protons, neutrons and electrons to the hydrogen atom resulted in the creation of all existing elements today.

As we can see, the secret behind the prolific multiplication of life forms is an intelligent process of shuffling and rearranging the same basic stuff - subatomic particles - into different combinations. All created things are manufactured on such a cosmic 'assembly line'. In the words of Arne Wyller, "every single hydrogen atom in our bodies was once part of the Big Bang itself", and forty percent of our atoms are "recycled stardust", originating inside the burning interior of the stars.[10]

When we look below the surface of our material world, we are faced with an irrevocable fact, that all life is made of the same 'thing'. All there is - you, me, plants, animals, the universe - is wearing exactly the same fabric of life. Creation, no matter how diversified, is nothing other than the *'flesh of God'* - in many physical disguises.

1. The Flesh of God

Phantoms of Light?

The further the investigation into the subatomic layers of matter the more paradoxical the outcome. Contrary to our normal perception, scientific research indicates that more than 99 percent of our familiar, solid world consists of empty space, including all living creatures. Theoretically speaking, "if the whole human body were compressed to nuclear density it would not take up more space than a pinhead."[11]

This may sound strange, but if we take a close look at the atoms which comprise physical matter, we encounter extremely small units surrounded almost entirely by empty space. Practically all of an atom's mass is contained within a tiny nucleus which is one one-hundred-thousandth of the whole thing! "To see the nucleus", says the theoretical physicist F. Capra, "we would have to blow up the atom to the size of the largest dome in the world, the dome of St Peter's Cathedral in Rome. In an atom of that size, the nucleus would be the size of a grain of salt!"[12]

If we take for granted what scientists are saying, then what, in fact, are we? Are we just empty ghostly creatures, phantoms of light in a virtual 3-D phantasmagoria of life? According to the leading scientists of our century - quantum physicist David Bohm and neurophysiologist Karl Pribram - the whole universe is fundamentally empty, an infinite dancing hologram of light. Working independently of one another, they both came to similar conclusions, which led them to the formulation of the holographic paradigm of reality. According to this model, the whole universe is a wavelike phenomenon, an infinite ocean of waves and frequencies which our brains convert holographically into the familiar images of the world in which we live.

The recent invention of holograms demonstrates most vividly how invisible light waves literally weave themselves into visible three-dimensional images. In the scientific world a hologram serves as a perfect scientific model of creation as a light construct. It is an optical illusion, a virtual image concocted from light waves. Even though it looks real, it is fundamentally empty. If you try touching it, your hand will encounter a void. What causes such an illusory image to appear as a real object is so-called interference: light waves criss-crossing and creating intricate wave patterns when they pass through each other. To visualize this, think of how dropping pebbles into a pond results in ripples of expanding concentric circles which create unusual patterns on the surface of the water when they run into each other.

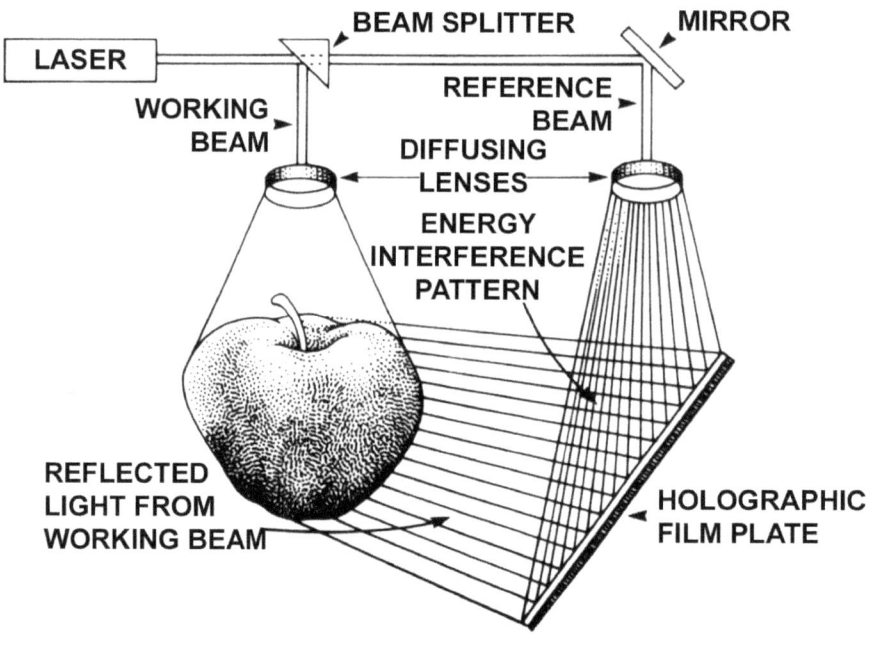

Creation of a Hologram

1. The Flesh of God

Light is the sole 'ingredient' of a hologram. The formula for its creation is the splitting of a single laser beam into two beams so that they can interweave into a desired holographic image. In order to split the beam it is sent through a device known as a beam-splitter. The first beam illumines and bounces off the object, for example an apple, being photographed. The second beam is directed to a holographic plate where both beams criss-cross, creating intricate patterns on the plate. When a bright light source shines through it, a three-dimensional image of the original apple reappears. This briefly sums up the art of making holograms.[13]

Pixelate, Blend, Emboss!

Everything in the universe is wavelike in nature. All subatomic particles which comprise matter are dimensionless, wavelike phenomena which create interference patterns when they collide with one another. The total space of the universe is flooded with a variety of waves invisible to the human eye: light waves, radio waves, X-rays and gamma rays constantly criss-crossing, creating interference patterns. Our perception of the world would be quite different if it wasn't for the ability of the mind to analyze and convert those wave patterns into real life images.

The process of image recognition begins in our eyes and is called stereoscopic vision, with both eyes participating in the process of perception.[14] If you look at an object with first one eye shut and then the other, you will find that the image seen by each eye differs slightly. Assessing those differences and computing the depth and position of external objects in space, the brain builds three-dimensional images by overlapping the views coming from the left and the right eye to the retinas. It literally fuses them into a single image.

This whole process, from perception to recognition of objects, takes place in the form of light signals. When light beams bounce off external objects, they enter the eyes through the pupil and strike hundreds of millions of photo-detectors inside the curved surface of the eyeball. As nerve signals, generated light information travels through the network of optical nerves to the brain for information processing. According to Pribram our brains are capable of creating internal three-dimensional holograms. The extremities of the brain's nerve cells look like tree branches tightly positioned next to each other. When electrical nerve currents pass through them they radiate outward in a wavelike motion. Pribram proposes that these expanding ripples are creating interference patterns, giving the brain its holographic properties.[15]

Perhaps you have had the opportunity of seeing a 3-D movie. In order to achieve the effect you needed to wear 3-D glasses. What you saw was just a stream of frequencies coming from the projector that were translated into three-dimensional imagery when filtered through the lens of the glasses. Without them, you would not have been able to enjoy the 3-D experience.

Similarly, according to the holographic model of the universe, we are participating in a never-ending 3-D movie of Life, except that the 3-D glasses are built in, so to speak. Our senses are sophisticated sensors equipped with lenses which enable us to experience the texture of reality. Figuratively speaking, our eyes, just like a filter, 'pixelate', 'blend', 'emboss', 'sharpen' and add depth to the influx of waves, converting them into three-dimensional images. Scientific experiments are leading to the belief that our other senses - taste, touch, hearing and smell - function similarly, analyzing and converting wavelike frequencies through their characteristic sensory filters. Each is a piece of the puzzle, adding to the total 'feel' of reality.

Pribram is not saying, "there aren't china cups or grains of beach sand out there. It simply means that a china cup has two very different aspects to its reality. When it is filtered through the lens of the brain it manifests as a cup. But if we could get rid of our lenses, we'd experience it as an interference pattern. Which one is real and which is illusion?"[16]

1. The Flesh of God

Why Spoil the Fun?

In theory, science has greatly modified our commonly accepted notions about the physical reality. But in practice, with the effects of three-dimensionality and solidity of matter being so profoundly genuine, we are easily fooled into believing that what we see, taste or touch is 'real' in a material sense. This 'realness' of creation is so hypnotically flawless that no living creature can escape the illusion. Without realizing it, all our thoughts, actions and desires are conditioned by this phenomenon.

Awakening from this trance state was held very high among the mystics on the spiritual path. 'Maya' is the famous Hindu term for the 'veil of illusion' which cloaks the true nature of reality. Therefore 'seeing through' it was a most desired spiritual attainment. Historical Buddha is one example of a rare person who awoke from the hypnotic state induced by 'maya', attaining enlightenment by realizing the true nature of reality.

And yet we could ask ourselves: why awaken at all? Why spoil the fun? Isn't the experience of 'realness' the beauty and pleasure of life anyway? Take the effect away and the play is over, lights come on in the 3-D cinema of life! How else would it be possible for us to touch, taste and enjoy life if it wasn't tangible and concrete in time and space?

The sensory experience of the material world is undeniably the genius of a creative, unlimited intelligence. But there is a negative side effect which comes with it, justifying the need for 'awakening' to our true nature.

The Separation Syndrome

Our senses play a vital role in facilitating the experience of being in the physical dimension. For a moment imagine shutting off all your senses, including your mind. All dividing lines between self and other would be dissolved. Your whole being would immediately turn into a mass of undifferentiated Oneness. Switch the senses on again and you are back in the physical dimension. The separation between self and other automatically returns.

This *Separation Syndrome* is a natural attribute of the physical dimension, just like shine is a natural attribute of the sun. In order for a sensory experience to take place, there must be a division between the *experiencer* and the *experienced*. Otherwise there is no *experience*. Separation is a fundamental feature of sensory perception, enabling us to taste, touch, smell, hear and see the world as something 'real', existing out there in its own right and identity. In that sense, there is nothing wrong with separation per se because it is a precondition for the material experience. It provides us with an opportunity to immerse ourselves in the beauty and the miracle of the physical dimension, to enjoy all those wonderful little things that life has to offer.

However, animosity and alienation amongst people are almost unavoidable, negative by-products of the Separation Syndrome. They occur because we confuse our sensory perceptions with reality. In other words the physical qualities of matter, such as solidity and three-dimensionality, are miscomprehended as the fundamental nature of the physical world, whereas they are only effects facilitated by our senses which convey the experience of materiality. Our true nature is essentially more subtle than solid, more spiritual than material, and often difficult to see through without conscious effort. It is closer to the truth to say that we are 'electrical force fields' rather than 'physical bodies'.

When we lack this awareness and our mentality is slanted towards a materialistic

1. The Flesh of God

worldview, a sense of separation is born in our hearts and minds. We act it out by drawing sharp dividing lines between *you* and *me*, *yours* and *mine* - by focusing our existence around *my* personal interests, *my* possessions, *my* sensual gratification, *my* success. Because of this limited perception, we fail to understand that there is really no substantial ground for separation or the selfish pursuits of the ego.

If the definition of "mine" implies something which a person has created from scratch, then nothing really belongs to us. When we say "I" or "mine", it has meaning only within a relative scope of existence - it is essentially just a human convention. We are not the creators of our body since we had no conscious participation or decision-making power in its conception, growth and birth. Most of our biological functions, such as breathing, blood circulation or digestion are involuntary. We have no conscious, personal control over these processes during our lifetime and yet our survival and well-being depends totally on them.

We have not created the ground we walk on, the air we breathe or the foods to sustain our bodies. Just like everything else in the observable universe, we are Nature's creations. Whatever our pursuits or activities, we are 'co-creating', using and shaping Nature's resources which are already available, in order to produce our human works. For example, hair grows naturally, we shape it into a creative style; foods ripen to perfection, we prepare them for delicious meals. Life as we know it is for the most part a product of forces beyond our personal domain. If all that is not ours were to be withdrawn from us, nothing would remain to call our own or take pride in. A separate ego-self is just an illusion, a façade.

Without some understanding of our true nature, the Separation Syndrome is a perfect breeding ground for suffering. It can lead to egoism and extreme materialism. The ruthless fulfillment of personal desires is at the core of all violence and hatred. It has culminated in an unprecedented potential for mass destruction and even extinction of the human race. If you stop and think for a moment, most of our suffering is humanly induced. It comes from hurting and destroying each other, through showing lack of love and care - behavior symptoms caused by the sense of separation.

Of course, the Separation Syndrome would not lead to suffering if our sensory perceptions were balanced with a greater understanding of how we truly operate on the material plane. In that case, it is possible to participate in the physical dimension while uninterruptedly staying 'on-line' with the source of primordial Oneness, aware that we are really not separate but one. A balanced view of matter and Spirit, body and mind, promotes harmony and inspires spiritual qualities of love, compassion, tolerance and mutual understanding. But unless we are willing to invest conscious effort to re-ignite the sense of Oneness within us, materialistic and egotistical attitudes will prevail. True spiritual progress of mankind can only be attained by reclaiming what has been lost: our link to Oneness.

The seduction of the senses is a powerful force to deal with and yet without it the earthly plane would lose its allure. In other words, if the sensory magic weren't so convincing and too easy to see through, we wouldn't be able to experience the miracle of Creation in its full expression. However, the sensory fiesta of life is a two-edged sword which can wound us deeply. The only way to avoid this is by complementing our sensory perception with a transcendental perception of our subtle, spiritual nature. When we say 'transcendental' we are alluding to the wave-nature of reality - as proposed by the holographic paradigm.

We can regain our lost sense of wholeness by bringing these two opposite poles, or angles, of viewing the same reality into balance with each other. Otherwise one-sided perception tips the cosmic scales out of balance and sets in motion the mechanism of suffering. The root of all human suffering lies in the discrepancy between our true nature, and our one-sided sensory perception of it. This problem has inhibited our spiritual growth and evolution for thousands of years. It is the 'achilles heel' of humanity.

1. The Flesh of God

Reclaiming our link to Oneness necessitates deep understanding of our true nature and so our quest for Oneness begins with that inquiry.

The Path

1. Our True Nature

1. Our True Nature

> *" [There] is disparity between the way things appear and the way they actually are. What appears as some kind of autonomous, objective reality does not really fit with the actual nature of reality... [A]lthough certain types of mental states seem so real, and although objects appear to be so vivid, in reality they are mere illusions. They do not exist in the way we think they do. [...] Our insight into emptiness will, of course, help us to understand that any ideas that are based on the contrary view, that things exist intrinsically and independently, are misapprehensions. They are misunderstandings of the true nature of reality."*
>
> A Simple Path
> His Holiness, The Dalai Lama

Yin and Yang of Creation

Scientists have discovered that light has a complementary nature: it is wavelike and particle-like at the same time. This means that it behaves as a stream of particles localized in space - at other times as a stream of waves spread out over vast regions. These two logically opposed yet complementary aspects of light are known as the 'wave-particle duality', one of the most important concepts in quantum physics.

In addition to light, the whole universe can be described in terms of such complementarity. Without exception, from subatomic particles to all types of waves such as gamma rays, X-rays or electromagnetic rays, the totality of creation exists in a paradoxically dual mode: as waves and as particles. This is known as Bohr's Complementarity Principle.[17]

Experiments have further demonstrated that it is impossible to observe both complementary aspects simultaneously. Depending on how scientists set up their measuring devices, they could either see the particle aspect or the wave aspect of matter but never both at the same time. Evidently dualistic Mother Nature is playing hide-and-seek, willing to show us only one of her sides at a time. According to Heisenberg's Uncertainty Principle[18] this is not related to the limitations of the experimental measuring apparatus; it simply means that no matter how we approach this, we can never see the 'particle-picture' and the 'wave-picture' of matter simultaneously. And yet only both of those aspects joined together give us a complete picture of reality.

The phenomenon of complementarity can be observed throughout the macro- and microcosm, from galactic proportions all the way down to the subatomic world. Light-dark, male-female, body-mind, particle-antiparticle are examples of an infinite spectrum of polar opposites which make up the fabric of the universe. Being a universal law, complementarity is exalted in Eastern mysticism and philosophy. The Chinese poles of Yin and Yang, or the divine couple Shiva and Shakti from Hindu mythology, are famous spiritual symbols of complementarity.

Nature pulsates in perfect rhythmic oscillations between her poles. It is the eternal heartbeat; it perpetuates motion and life and holds the universe together in a state of perfect equilibrium. Complementing each other, polar opposites exist in a dynamic state of balance. The middle line of symmetry between the poles represents the axis of Nature. We resonate in harmony with her rhythms when we are able to maintain a balance between all extremes.

1. Our True Nature

Windows into Transcendence

Like icing on the cake, our senses put a 'glaze' over our wave body, making us look and feel physical. However, according to the Complementarity Principle, this represents only one of these two faces of reality. The physical or 'particle-picture' of reality is continually reinforced by our senses, dominating our existence, while the other aspect is pushed into the background.

We feel very much at home in our physical disguise, often forgetting that overemphasis on the material aggravates the Separation Syndrome. It deepens our sense of separation, increasing egotistical and aggressive tendencies which can lead to a great deal of suffering. In order to avoid such pitfalls it is imperative to seek a balanced perception of life in general. In other words, we must live with a complete picture of reality, not just its material half. Developing a more intimate relationship with the transcendental, wavelike nature of reality brings us closer to the experience of Oneness and neutralizes our feelings of separation. It brings us in harmony with Universal Law.

We naturally trust our eyes. We tend to believe that what we see is fact. Being hidden from our eyes, the idea of a transcendental reality is difficult to grasp with the intellect. The advantage of Holographic Meditation techniques lies in working to alter our visual perception. This is a highly effective way of conveying the idea, enabling us to capture the essence of transcendence with the naked eye. With the help of a visual technique called Hologazing, we can see thought-provoking 'holographic' imagery emerging before our eyes during a meditation session.

With this imagery, complex scientific and metaphysical descriptions of Nature's laws are translated into simple visual analogies which we can more easily relate to. For example, seeing solid objects turn into transparent images becomes an 'encounter of a quantum kind', sheer transcendence staring us in the face. Scraping the glaze from the windows, we look inside the 'House of Transcendence' and what we see is solid objects turning into a thin veil, an ethereal membrane between form and emptiness.

Capturing the essence of transcendence, these meditations serve as a bridge between the seemingly irreconcilable material and spiritual worlds. The physical and the transcendental half of reality are sewn evenly together into an integral worldview. Correcting our worldview at this most fundamental level is necessary for the attainment of inner balance and wholeness in our existence. It represents the first logical step toward happiness.

The Mind's Eye

In a series of three meditation exercises called *True Nature Meditations*, we are brought closer to our transcendental, wave-nature with every step, until balance between the dual aspects of reality is re-established. They are called True Nature Meditations because they facilitate deep understanding of the true make-up of reality. They should not be viewed separately but as three stages of progressively peeling the layers from matter. They provide us with an opportunity to view solid objects in a way they don't ordinarily appear to us. Through the HM viewfinder (see 'Hologazing' on page 35), we are able actually to observe solid, physical objects 'melt down' and become 'non-material'. They assume ethereal qualities and behave in ways in which we don't normally expect them to behave.

This is due to the fact that what we perceive as physical reality is created in a rather mysterious collaboration between our sensory organs and mind. For example, when we say that we are seeing an object we are actually perceiving only the light signals reflected from it. The object is truly just an abstract current of frequencies which enter

1. Our True Nature

our eyes and travel through a network of optic nerves to our brains, where they are finally translated into real life imagery. Considering the fact that light signals reflected from all over the place are bombing our eyes and traveling to our brains simultaneously, it becomes more than obvious that an intelligence of the mind is involved in the process of sorting out so many frequencies into a recognizable reality.

With the practice of these meditations, we become more familiar with the holographic nature of our visual perception. As previously stated, our eyes and mind display holographic properties. We have a sense of depth and three-dimensionality because the images perceived by each eye separately are 'holographically' blended into a single image when they overlap. The distance between our eyes is approx. $2^{1/2}$ inches. The right eye sees slightly differently from the left. When both images are superimposed in the visual field, a fusion of the two views occurs in the brain and results in the 'parallax', the formation of a 3-D image.[19]

A single eye is also capable of providing us with three-dimensional views because it is never absolutely still, taking a multitude of snapshots by slightly moving around a pivotal point in the center of the eye. These subtly differing images are sent to the brain and fused into a 3-D image, similar to the functioning of two eyes. It is due to the overlapping (interference) of layers coming from both eyes that images leap into three-dimensionality and assume material qualities. As we shall see in the following pages, the HM meditation techniques provide us with direct insight into this profound relationship between the eyes and the mind, and how they facilitate 3-D effects to create an experience of 'physicality'.

Based on studies of the evolution of language, the eyes were not always capable of perceiving the whole spectrum of colors. First came red and black and later on the ability to perceive other colors slowly emerged.[20] The slow development of color sense is one example of our gradual evolution of consciousness. It means that when a concept is born in the mind, it becomes a manifest reality outside.

In the same way, developing a better sense for our transcendental 'wave nature' represents an evolutionary step in our spiritual growth, in that the soul has been able to pierce through the veil of the senses. The flexibility of shifting the lens of the physical eyes corresponds to the flexibility of the inner lens of the mind. Since the eyes are the physical counterpart of the spiritual mind's eye, it symbolizes the emergence of a whole new mental faculty. In that sense, engaging in the practice of True Nature Meditations also signifies a state of mind rather than just a mastery of techniques.

Unified Awareness

Many people have their lens of perception 'rusted' in one setting: it is stuck in 'solid mode'. It takes a powerful spiritual lubricant to make it mobile and flexible again so that it can glide back and forth between the wave and the particle mode of reality. True Nature Meditations are built on visual exercises designed to flex and lubricate the lens of the mind so that it can slide more smoothly between these two polar settings. Getting it 'unstuck' re-establishes the lost balance.

I am the particle, I am the wave. I am the body, I am the mind. I am the wave in the highest sense, an electrical force field, but by virtue of sensory perception I am also a material body. Both are true. Once our lens of perception is working in its dual capacity again, we are capable of perceiving ourselves as both material and spiritual beings. When both pictures of reality are equally represented without mutually excluding each other, we have establish a balanced perception of life in general. In the philosophy of Holographic Meditation, this auspicious state of mind is called Unified Awareness.

It is difficult to alter our deeply ingrained ideas about the world we live in. True Nature Meditations represents a short cut in reprogramming our conventional perception of reality by providing us with an alternative perception that we are not accus-

1. Our True Nature

tomed to. Witnessing this radical visual imagery with just the naked eye softens our rigid perceptions, making us more 'porous' as individuals. The whole world cheered ecstatically when the Berlin Wall was torn down because it symbolized the re-unification of two peoples. The ultimate message of these meditations is for each one of us to tear down our 'Berlin Wall' of separation which we have erected within us, due to our one-sided perception of reality.

A greater infusion of transcendental awareness enables us to regain the lost feeling of Oneness with our world. The narrow definition of 'I am' expands into the notion of 'I am the world'. As the sharp, solid outlines of the outside world melt away, we are no longer so burdened by separation. On the contrary, grasping how creation is 'holographically' orchestrated into tangible, external forms - every thing, every person, every blade of grass - becomes an altar to the genius of creative intelligence. Our sense of wonder returns and we see the beauty and the mystery of creation in a whole new light. The grandeur of Creation's divine design fills us with the newly-found bliss of being a part of such a miracle.

Some of us may feel that giving up our customary perception of reality is a threat to the ego. Let us not forget that the real threat is that of war, nuclear and ecological destruction, corruption, moral degradation and many other negative expressions of the Separation Syndrome which are rooted in ignorance of our true nature. It is much less painful to grow consciously by changing our worldview, rather than unconsciously being forced to learn from often fatal mistakes.

SENSORY PERCEPTION ⇩ SENSE OF SEPARATION ⇩ EGOISM, GREED, HATRED, VIOLENCE, CORRUPTION, EXTREME MATERIALISM (NEGATIVE EXPRESSIONS OF THE SEPARATION SYNDROME) ⇩ PHYSICAL, MENTAL, EMOTIONAL PAIN, DESTRUCTION AND MANY OTHER FORMS OF HUMANLY INDUCED SUFFERING, ROOTED IN SEPARATION	TRANSCENDENTAL PERCEPTION ⇩ SENSE OF ONENESS ⇩ COMPASSION, LOVE, TOLERANCE, MUTUAL UNDERSTANDING, HUMANITARIAN ACTION ⇩ ELIMINATION OF SUFFERING CAUSED BY THE SEPARATION SYNDROME GREATER HAPPINESS AND FULFILLMENT IN LIFE

SENSORY PERCEPTION + TRANSCENDENTAL PERCEPTION = UNIFIED AWARENESS

Sensory perception promotes a feeling of separation, Transcendental perception one of unity. In order to develop a well-rounded, balanced worldview, both perceptions of reality must be equally represented in a person's life. Unified Awareness is a state of Oneness with all creation despite the sense of separation.

1. Our True Nature

The Art of Hologazing

Hologazing is a rather simple visual technique with dynamics similar to those of the photographic lens zooming in and out, on selected objects, for close-up or long distance shots. In fact, the way the human eye sees things is completely analogous to a camera. Our pupils function just like a lens automatically operated by the brain and the set of muscles in each eye. In order to avoid blurry images, it focuses the light with great precision on the retina.

In our normal way of seeing the eyes 'zoom' onto a selected object, as if they were photographing a close-up of it. In order to change this into Hologazing mode, the eyes are made to zoom away from the selected object into the distance. Our total perception changes dramatically simply by adjusting the 'zoom lens' within the eye.

Hologazing can best be described as looking at close-up objects while the lens of the eyes is set to distant viewing mode. In other words, you bring an object up to your eyes as if you want to examine it very closely, but instead of looking at it directly you relax your eyes and just gaze through it into the distance. Because the object is so close to your visual field you are still looking at it, only indirectly. As soon as this is done, the object changes its original form and an unusual 'holographic' imagery starts emerging. When you think of it, this is the opposite of what anybody would do in normal circumstances. Nobody brings an object up close as if they wish to examine it, only to not look at it. But right there a rare window of opportunity opens up, and Nature begins to reveal some of her innermost secrets.

The Path

Wave Nature Meditation

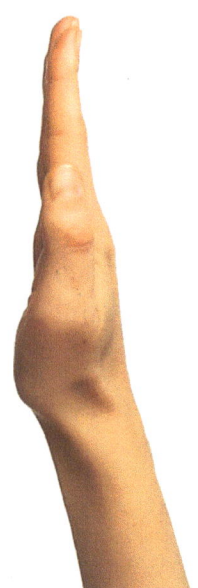

1. Hold one hand upright, with palm sideways. Your hand should be directly in front of your eyes, approximately 10 inches away from your face.

2. Now apply the Hologazing technique. With that hand in the same position, shift your focus and 'gaze through' your hand at the wall in the background. (A neutral background is recommended as an optimum backdrop for observing this imagery.) Witness the doubling effect of the hand, as well as the fact that it assumes a transparent, wavelike appearance.

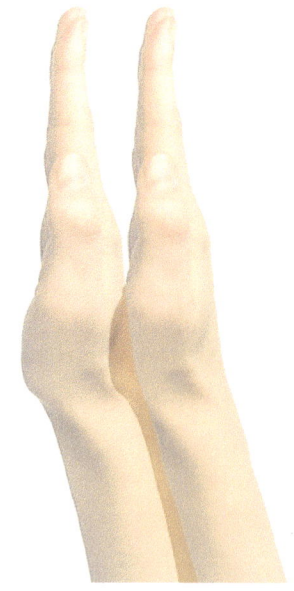

1. Our True Nature

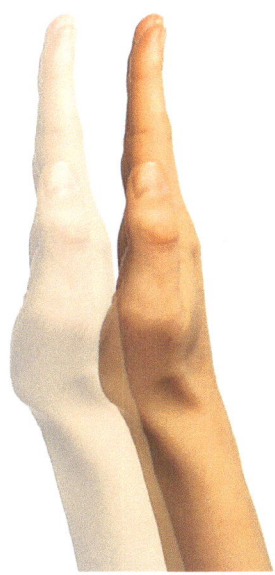

3. Continue gazing steadily through your hand for several minutes. Observe the 'double' hand oscillating back and forth, sometimes appearing opaque and sometimes transparent. At times, the hand will momentarily completely vanish from sight.

WAVE NATURE MEDITATION is a visual analogy of matter as a wavelike phenomenon. In this exercise, we are looking closely at what happens to our hand when viewed in the holomode. We discover that it changes its solid appearance into a wavelike or ghostly double image. It becomes a thin veil, a transparent layer through which we can see the total background.

How can we explain this effect? Evidently a single, solid image of the hand is disunited into two independent transparent images. As previously stated, in the normal process of 'stereoscopic vision', images from both eyes are fused into a single one. Here we are observing the reverse process, whereby the hand assumes a wavelike quality.

As we continue to meditate on the imagery we observe another unusual phenomenon: the double 'phantom' hand behaves like a flickering candle. It is transparent until it vanishes, leaving no trace of its existence. Then it reappears. This 'wave-particle dance' continues for as long as we choose to observe it. In accordance with the dual nature of matter, the hand appears sometimes as a particle-picture and sometimes as a wave-picture of reality, rhythmically oscillating back and forth between these two modes. This imagery is a perfect layman's model for the 'wave-particle duality'.

If we move our eyes around while keeping the hand in a steady position, the visual effect remains intact. Even if we move the hand slowly to the left and right across the face, we can still see the complete background through it. We would expect the hand to obscure the background but that is not the case. The emerging visuals are not caused by crossing the eyes or in some other unnatural way, but rather by simply changing the depth of our perception. Is our hand really just a wavelike, phantom image which our mind converts into a solid-looking hand, as indicated by the 'holographic paradigm'?

Observing this imagery reprograms our ordinary perception by deepening an awareness of the transcendental aspect of nature.

Note: Try this exercise: close one eye and perform the same experiment as indicated above. You will see that the hand obscures parts of the background as you move it back and forth across your visual field. The hand behaves in accordance with what we logically expect to take place. To understand this phenomenon better, let's try the next meditation exercise.

1. Our True Nature

Holographic Nature Meditation

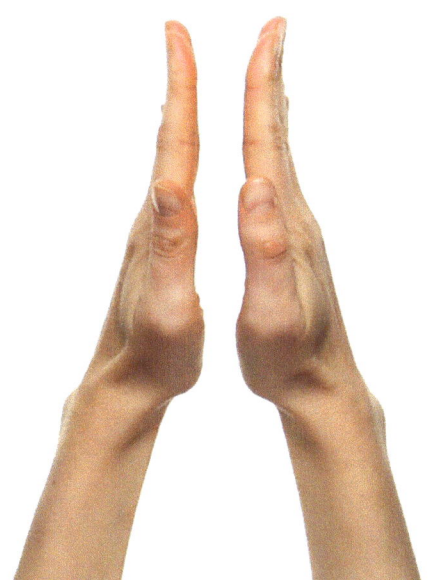

1. Turn your hands to face each other, approximately $1/3$ inches apart.

2. Apply the Hologazing technique, zooming into the distance, and witness the doubling effect and wavelike appearance of the hands. Observe the creation of a virtual shape in the middle where the wavelike images of both hands converge.

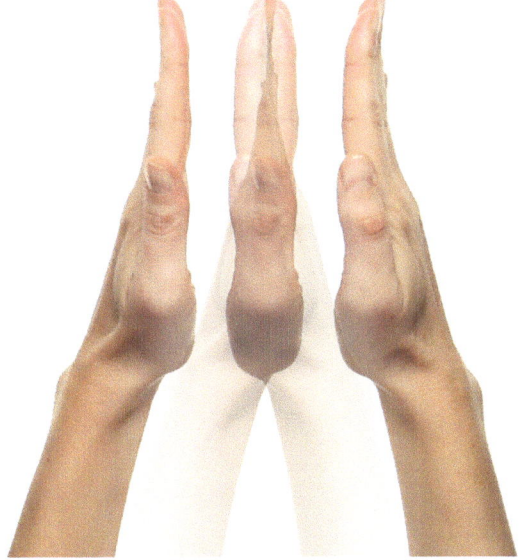

HOLOGRAPHIC NATURE MEDITATION is a home version of a holographic laboratory, enabling us to observe with our own eyes the rather mysterious process of 'creatio ex nihilo' - a virtual, holographic image springing out of thin air. Even though the virtual shape is not solid in the physical sense, it assumes some degree of realness. For example, if you try looking through this virtual shape you will notice it actually obscures things in the background, just as any other solid object does.

The holographic phenomenon called 'interference' has a perfect visual analogy in this imagery. When Hologazing at our hands, both the left and right hand change their normal solid appearance into double wavelike shapes. As soon as we bring both hands together an inch or less apart, so that their wavelike fields become superimposed, then illusory, three-dimensional shapes appear before our eyes. In other words, virtual images are created through an 'interference' process.

Beside the hands, we can experiment with any solid objects as long as they are not wider than an inch or so. This has to do with the dynamics of 'stereoscopic vision', particularly the distance between the eyes, which is two-and-a-half inches. If the objects we are observing are wider than one inch or so, the left and right visual fields overlap completely, fusing them into one solid-looking image, as we are used to perceiving.

This is why we cannot observe this imagery with one eye only, even though it functions holographically. The objects would have to be extremely small in order for us to observe the diffusion of a single image.

1. Our True Nature

Complementary Nature Meditation

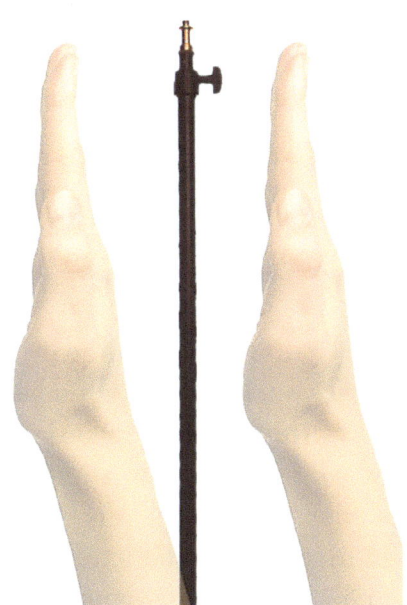

1. Hold one hand vertically with the palm sideways. Hold it in front of your eyes, approximately 10 inches away. Now apply Hologazing. Look through that hand into the distance, at a selected object in the background. (You can choose any object as long as it is not wider than an inch). Witness the doubling of the original solid shape of the hand as well as it assuming a transparent, wavelike appearance.

2. Change your focus once again, looking directly at that hand. Notice how it returns to its normal solid appearance, while the object turns into a double image and assumes a wavelike appearance. Go slowly back and forth several times, alternating your focus between your hand and the object.

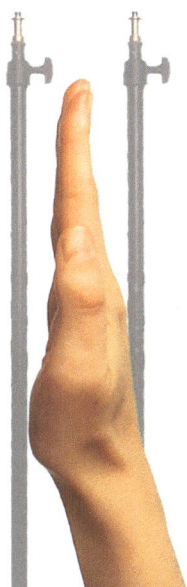

COMPLEMENTARY NATURE MEDITATION faithfully simulates Heisenberg's Uncertainty Principle. If we focus our eyes directly on the hand in the foreground, it looks solid and material as we normally perceive it. But as soon as we change our focus to the object in the background, the hand shifts its solid appearance into a wavelike or ghostly double image. It becomes transparent and we can see the whole background through it. Depending on whether we choose to look at the hand directly or indirectly, by gazing through it into the distance it changes from a solid to a wavelike image. The fact is that depending on our perception, the hand exists in ordinary, solid form if we choose to observe it. But if we choose not to observe it then it dissolves into a 'phantom' hand. Which one is real and which is an illusion?

So there is an obvious analogy between the imagery we are observing in this meditation and Heisenberg's Uncertainty Principle. The eyes operate through a set of muscles adjusting their lens, which ultimately is the lens of the mind. Depending on how we set up our measuring device - in this case the eye's lens - the hand sometimes appears to us as a wavelike image, sometimes as a solid one. Just as the Uncertainty Principle states, we can only observe the solid particle-picture or the wave-picture of the hand, but never both at the same time. Our role as observer is of fundamental importance because our choice of perception becomes the fine line between its 'existence' and 'non-existence'. This exercise reminds us that what we perceive as the outside world is not the absolute truth. Our perception and interpretation of reality greatly depend on how the senses and the mind measure it.

1. Our True Nature

Visual Koans

In Zen tradition, koans are commonly used as a tool for spiritual awakening. They are paradoxical questions which, through reflection, bring the student to a greater awareness. With great emphasis on visual imagery, True Nature Meditations play the role of visual koans for the mind. The word 'meditation' comes from the Latin word 'meditatio' and means 'to think deeply', 'to contemplate'. True Nature Meditations are meant to start a process of deep thinking and contemplation about our true nature.

Every time we engage in this practice, we are intersecting our ordinary flow of awareness by overriding our sensory perception and visually impressing the mind towards transcendence. By repetitiously taking snapshots of emerging holographic imagery we are gradually 'recalibrating' our mental patterns, deepening the awareness of our non-material wave nature. Therefore it is best if they are practiced as often as we can. Repetition is the key. It is not enough just to 'get' it once on an intellectual level. We reach ever-higher degrees of realization with regular practice.

Just like an empty battery, we must charge and recharge ourselves with transcendental awareness until we become saturated with it. Intellectual understanding doesn't suffice. This can be compared to an instruction manual teaching us how to charge a battery. But if we don't actually charge it, it remains dead and useless. In the same way, in order to transform our fundamental awareness we must infuse our whole being with it. Every single cell of our body-mind must become it, sinking deep into our unconscious. It is a gradual process, not something which ordinarily happens overnight.

The advantage of these meditations is that they are well suited even to people with busy lifestyles. Because of the simplicity of the techniques, they can be practiced anywhere and at any time - standing, sitting or lying down. Though longer, sitting meditations are encouraged, to have a mini-session it only takes raising the hand(s) and going into holomode for a few minutes. They can be practiced 'on the go', even when we are in a hurry. They are active, visual meditations which complement our fast-paced lifestyle. By repeatedly doing them many times during the day they become an integral part of our daily life. They make transcendence a household name.

When having a full session, follow these steps:

POSTURE: Sit in a comfortable position with your back straight and relaxed. If you are not an experienced meditator accustomed to sitting on the floor in a lotus position, sitting and leaning back in a chair is recommended, giving your spine enough support. Relax your arms on your lap.

BREATHING: The brain and breathing cycle are interconnected through the physiological mechanism of the voluntary and involuntary nervous systems. When the mind is agitated, breathing becomes irregular, shallow and agitated. Deepening and slowing down the breathing helps calm the mind and induce a meditative state. Close your eyes and begin your session with long, slow inhalations and exhalations. Relax. (5 min.)

CONCENTRATION: Depending on the type of meditation, bring your hand(s) into position and apply Hologazing. Focusing intently on the emerging imagery causes an instant centering of our mind. Practicing this easy exercise focuses the mind and gradually develops concentration powers. (2-5 min.)

MEDITATION: Close your eyes and think deeply about the meaning of transcendence conveyed by visual imagery. Every time you get distracted, bring yourself back to the main theme. Look closely at insights arising from within. During the final stage of the meditation session, as your mind empties of all thoughts you will be saturated with a profound feeling of Oneness. (20 min.)

Full sessions should last half an hour to an hour. They are recommended 2-3 times a week (or more if desired), in combination with frequent daily mini-sessions last-

1. Our True Nature

ing only a few minutes at a time. Always practice full sessions on an empty stomach in a clean, quiet place that is conducive to meditation.

Note: For any further clarification, contact the author.

2. Happiness

2. Happiness

Indra's Net of Pearls

Nature's laws govern our existence, and our well-being greatly depends on whether or not we live in harmony with them. It is therefore vital that we properly understand this deeper order of things and learn how to apply it toward greater happiness in life. For example, balance in Nature is a universal law. Just as gravity causes objects to fall to the ground, all things seek naturally to return to their 'ground state' - their point of balance. Being a part of Nature we are no exception. Whenever we violate this principle we organically attract certain conditions in life which propel us back into balance.

Even though everything in creation is in continual flux, constantly undergoing change, it never ends in chaos. For example, the four fundamental forces in the universe - gravity, electromagnetic, strong and weak forces - are perfectly orchestrated like clockwork. If there had been even the slightest upset of the equilibrium between them, creation wouldn't exist as we know it. After the Big Bang, if cosmic gravity had been a little stronger or a little weaker, creation would have either collapsed or been blown apart. If the earth had settled in its orbit a little closer or a little further away from the sun, organic life could not have evolved because there would have been too much heat or too much cold. Atoms could not have been created if the strong or the weak forces within their structures were not in perfect balance. As we can see, Nature as a whole displays perfect order, despite a certain degree of unpredictability.

Oneness, or the universal interconnectedness of all things, is another natural principle of vital importance in our quest for happiness. It tells us that we cannot effectively solve problems in life without treating them in relationship to the whole of existence. In Mahayana Buddhism, there is an ancient metaphor of the God Indra's net of pearls hanging over his palace, arranged in ways so that each individual pearl is reflected in all other pearls and in each pearl all others are reflected.[21] This symbolism alludes to the profound interconnectedness of all life. When the hologram was recently discovered, scientists realized that it was structured just as were Indra's net of pearls: when cut into pieces, each fragment of the hologram still displayed a picture of the whole.

The discovery of this holographic phenomenon was of fundamental importance to scientists, giving them the key to the paradoxical relationship between matter and energy. David Bohm used it as an analogy when developing his scientific theory of 'undivided wholeness'. It became his new model of the universe which he described as an unbroken, undivided totality. He envisioned the universe as a dynamic cosmic hologram which is involved in an unending process of movement and change, called 'holomovement'.[22]

The essence behind 'undivided wholeness' is that every part of creation is interconnected with every other part. Just as Bohm's 'holomovement' implies, the slightest change in one part of creation will automatically be felt in every other part. Think of

2. Happiness

the universe as an endless chain of 'flow charts'. Every time there is a change in one, all others throughout the cosmos will be accordingly reconfigured. If we translate this universal law to the personal level, it means that our every thought, emotion or action causes a chain reaction, affecting every single aspect of our life.

The Twelvefold Path

The goal of practicing True Nature Meditations is to bring our basic perception of the world into balance. Merging the solid and the wave-picture of reality in our mind represents our first gesture towards harmony with the Universal Law. It enables us to form a balanced worldview as our solid, healthy foundation for life. We call this integral state of mind Unified Awareness.

Our next step is to expand the meaning of Unified Awareness in relation to our everyday life. How does it actually reflect in our attitude, emotions and circumstances? What characterizes the person who has achieved Unified Awareness? How does he or she think, act, feel? How does it change his or her life for the better? Once we have the complete picture we can use it as a working model for life mastery. The idea is to transform all our character traits and behavior patterns which fundamentally clash with Unified Awareness, so we can fully integrate them into our daily lives.

In order to define the characteristics of Unified Awareness, it is necessary to dissect it. This is done according to the following 2-step HM formula.

I. When the totality of existence, as a single laser beam, is sent through the Prism of Life, it branches into four major levels: Thinking, Acting, Feeling and Materializing. These summarize the four basic forms of expression: 1) we think 2) we act 3) we feel and 4) we materialize through the physical dimension.

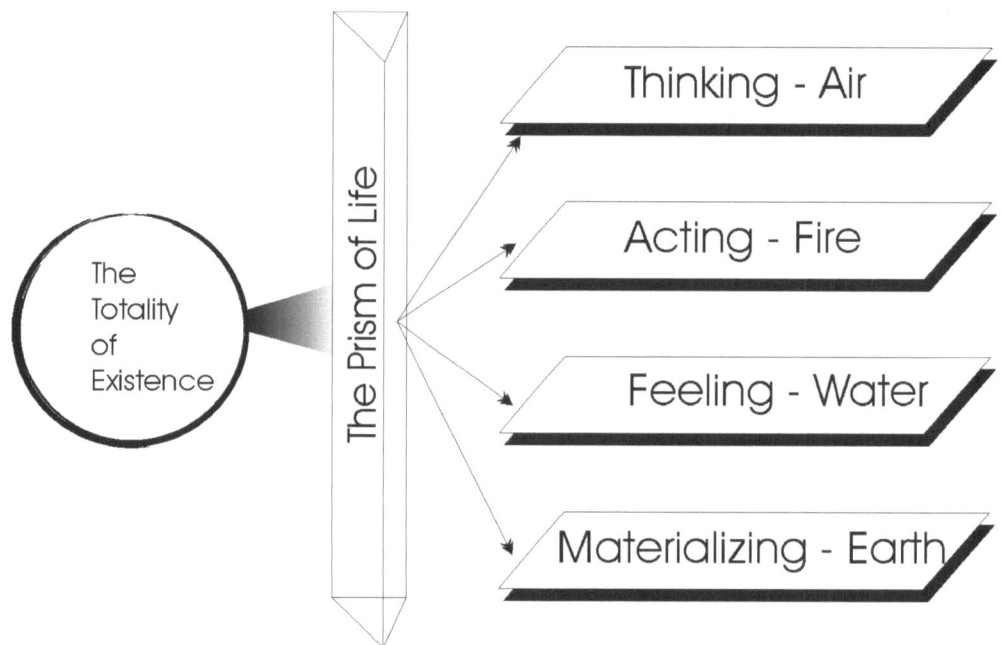

Air, Fire, Water and Earth are primary elements, symbolizing the four levels of density in which matter appears. Similarly, Thinking, Acting, Feeling and Materializing represent four different densities of awareness. Therefore the Thinking function is associated with Air, Acting with Fire, Feeling with Water and Materializing with the Earth element.

2. Happiness

II. The second step is to diffract Unified Awareness - as a single laser beam through the mind's lens - and see how it differentiates itself as it descends through these four basic levels. Initially Unified Awareness divides into three rays, or three different angles of reality perception: 1) positive polarity 2) negative polarity and 3) their synthesis. Thus, at the Thinking level, we obtain the first division into Spirit, Matter and Oneness.

Further diversification occurs when these rays of awareness continue diffracting through the descending levels of Acting, Feeling and Materializing. In the final analysis we obtain twelve fundamental principles, each being a different facet of Unified Awareness. So essentially, they are twelve derivatives from one single principle.

The following model gives us clarity about how Unified Awareness is expressed through four major levels of existence. It also shows us the map - the Twelvefold Path leading to the mastery of life.

THE PYRAMID OF UNIFIED AWARENESS

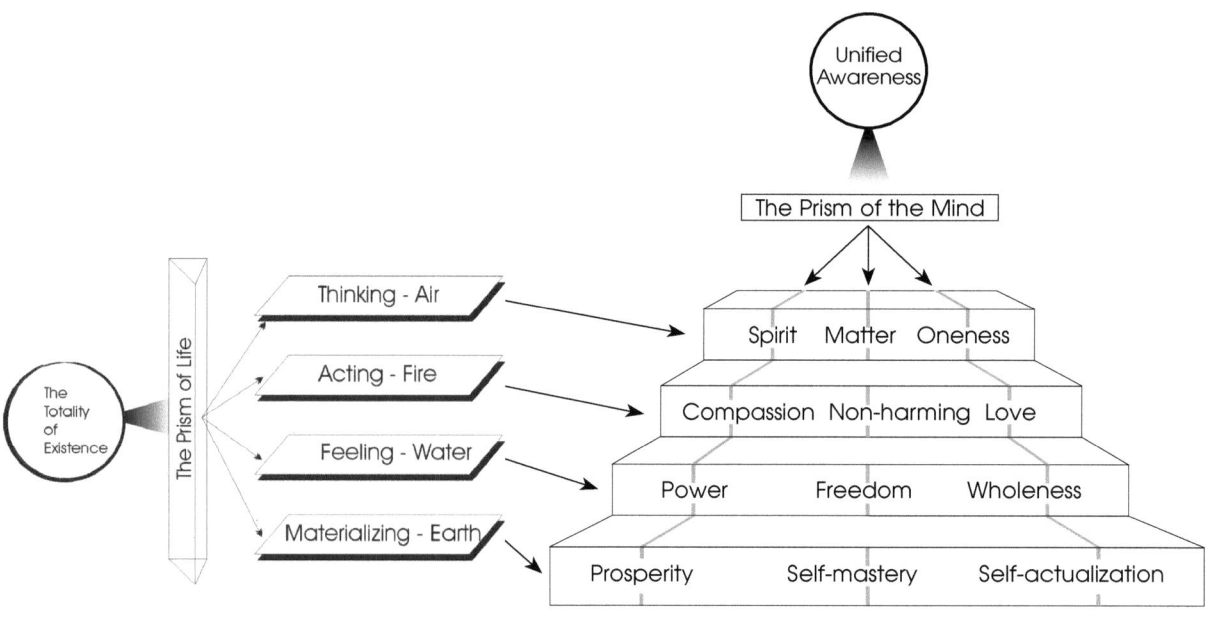

(Unified Awareness differentiates itself in descending levels, from a 'single principle')

2. Happiness

The Triads

How do I think?
What is my philosophy of life?

AIR TRIAD: PHILOSOPHY OF LIFE

SPIRIT, MATTER and ONENESS represent complex philosophical concepts of universal magnitude. Together they summarize the totality of existence. If we sincerely aspire toward realizing the true meaning of life, we cannot ignore these key concepts. They are indispensable in our search for knowledge, as well as for developing a sound philosophy of life.

The Triads

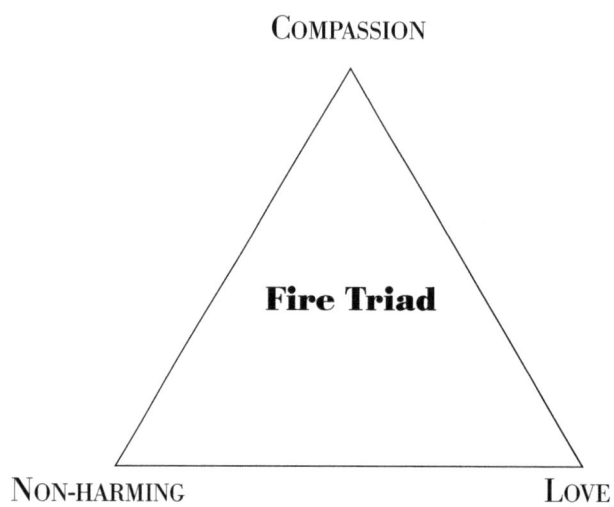

How do I act?
What ethical principles characterize my actions?

FIRE TRIAD: PERSONAL ETHICS

COMPASSION, NON-HARMING and LOVE are universal spiritual principles which form a healthy foundation for our actions and behavior. They bring definition to what is thought of as 'spiritually correct' action. If we want our dealings in life to be wholesome we must be able to understand and integrate these principles into the finest fabric of our awareness. When deeply ingrained through constant practice, these principles become a part of our nature, and spontaneously maintain their integrity through all our actions.

2. Happiness

The Triads

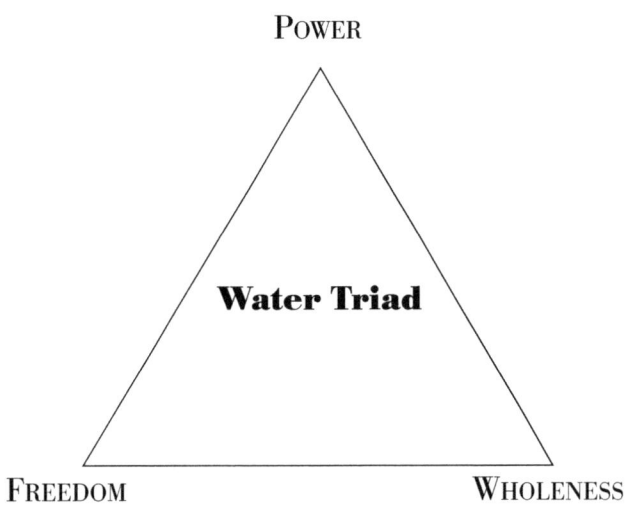

How do I feel?
What is my inner state of mind?

WATER TRIAD: INNER STATE OF MIND

POWER, FREEDOM and WHOLENESS are universal desires, and human happiness is often measured by their fulfillment. Their realization reflects a harmonious inner state of mind which we come to embody when in touch with our true nature. They form the basis for a balanced internal reality.

The Triads

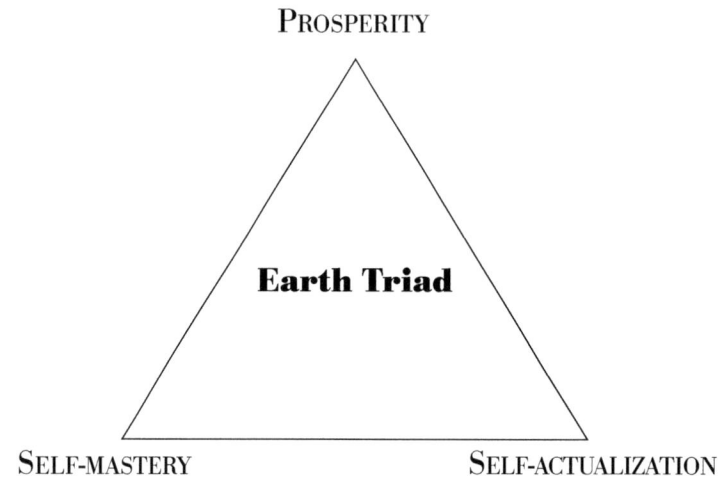

How do I materialize?
What are the concrete, tangible results of my life?

EARTH TRIAD: MATERIAL REALITY

PROSPERITY, SELF-MASTERY and SELF-ACTUALIZATION express the final crystallization of our multi-dimensional self on the material plane. They are the three mirrors which reflect and concretely measure who we have become. Through them the totality of our thoughts, actions and emotions are a tangible expression. The invisible has becomes visible.

2. Happiness

The Earth Mirrors the Sky!

Because of their complexity, the 12 principles are converted into meditation themes. Discovering their deepest meaning always has greater personal value when it comes as a result of our own seeking. We must bring it up from the very depths of our being through our own efforts. The 12 principles are called 'elixirs', indicating that once they have been mastered to perfection, they truly are the Elixirs of Life.

Just as a fruit that ripens slowly and then yields its sweetness, so is our awareness and character perfected through the practice of these meditations. Each meditation helps us to single out and work to master one principle of Unified Awareness at a time. This enables us to gradually weed out negative personal traits which conflict with the true meaning of Unified Awareness. If we are still prone to aggressive outbursts, if we are unethical, egotistical, judgmental or addicted, then we haven't really achieved the integration of Unified Awareness - the real purpose of meditating on the 12 principles. If we draw a parallel between it and a 12-stringed instrument, practicing these mediations would be like fine-tuning each principle (string) until perfect harmony (music) is achieved.

At the same time, this model of 12 principles gives us a holistic picture of what is required for the mastery of life. It reminds us that fulfillment at the material level is impossible without mastery of all other levels. Just as Bohm's 'undivided wholeness' implies, every aspect of our life is interconnected with every other aspect. So when we look at the four major levels of existence - Thinking, Acting, Feeling and Materializing - we realize that they are all related via an inner, causal relationship: our thoughts, initially on a very subtle vibratory level, solidify progressively into actions, feelings and finally concrete conditions.

In order to understand this better, take for example the idea '*house*' and see how it actually appears in four densities or forms of expression: 1) abstract thought 2) the spoken word 3) the written word (2-D image) and 4) the physical object (3-D image). The physical form of the house is the grossest form of the idea. Similarly, our life on the material plane is a condensation of all that we previously thought, did and felt. This plane is fertile soil, where the seeds of our thoughts take root and later become visible. Who we are inside is inherently reflected outside: in our physical appearance, in tangible circumstances, etc. There is never a discrepancy between above and below, inside and outside. Therefore, replacing a broken thing is only a superficial measure. We must see what caused it to break in the first place. In other words, we must trace our problems all the way to the root, which leads us to the top of the pyramid - the Thinking level.

The following is a simplified model showing the 'cascade' relationship between these four major levels of awareness:

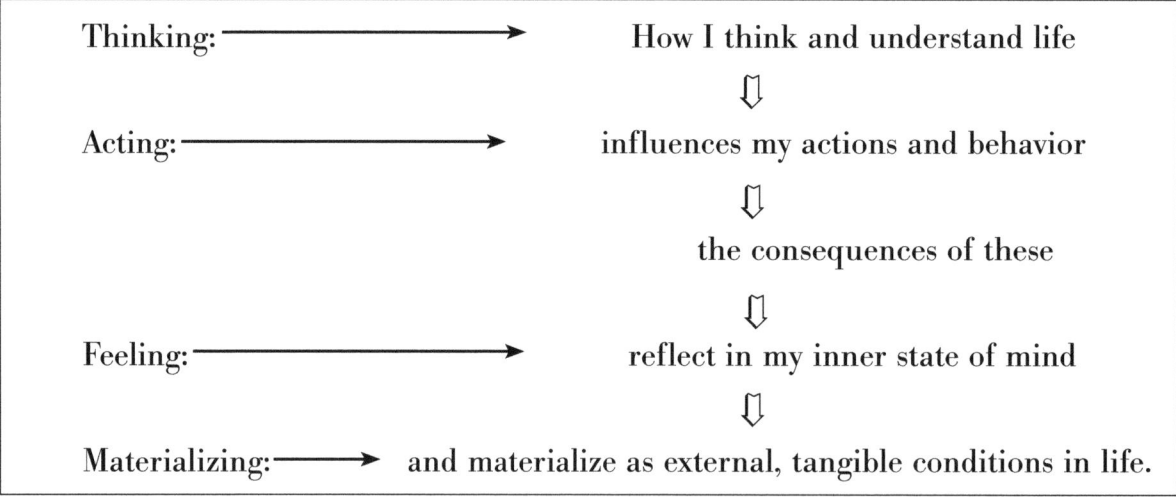

As above, so below!

2. Happiness

In the initial stages of our meditation practice we focus on mastering the principles from the Air Triad. The goal is to find and pull out the roots of our spiritually-deficient thought patterns which produce suffering in our life. After we have developed a healthy philosophy of life we can proceed with the Fire Triad, Water Triad, and finally the Earth Triad. Fulfillment on the material plane of awareness is impossible without the harmonization of all levels.

Corona

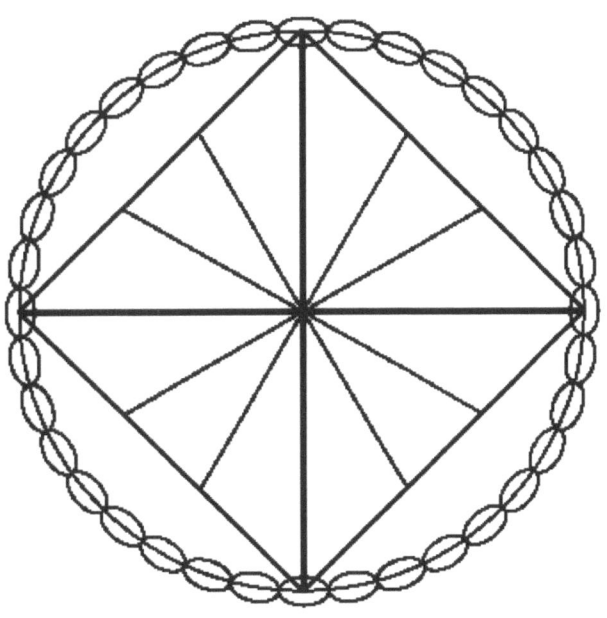

Corona

HM Symbol of Unified Awareness

Corona is a geometric diagram symbolizing the perfected state of mind called Unified Awareness. We could view it as a modern version of Buddha- or Christ-consciousness.

The circle symbolizes the uncreated, infinite spiritual realm within which everything is contained. In shape it resembles a 'standing wave', an electronic pattern surrounding the nucleus of an atom. This symbolizes the quantum jump, or the raising of consciousness, to the highest possible orbit of Unified Awareness which an individual can attain.

The diamond within the circle represents the materialization of the spiritual in the physical dimension.

The cross divides the diamond into four sections, marked by the four primary elements. They symbolize four modalities of existence. The midpoint where the infinite (the circle) and the finite (the diamond) merge alchemically, is the point of exaltation - the fifth element - symbolizing individual wholeness achieved through harmonization of all four components.

The number 3 represents Tri-unity or synthesis. It is the binding factor which re-integrates the preceding duality into a state of Perfection.

The number 4 is universally linked with the Earth and symbolizes Materialization.

The number 12 is a product of 3×4. As a round number of a full circle, it symbolizes Completion.

The relationship between the numbers 3, 4 and 12 can be translated into: the synthesis or Perfection (3) of Unified Awareness, when materialized (4) in practical life, it creates a full circle between spiritual and material qualities. It represents the final stage or Completion (12).

Thus spiritual mastery, applied fully in the context of material existence, leads to

2. Happiness

wholeness and greater personal happiness.

    The 12 principles of Unified Awareness are captured in a coherent system of 12 symbols, the theme of our next chapter.

3. If the Hands Could Talk

3. If the Hands Could Talk

> *"Symbols may appear in one place - in fact, they may be buried for centuries, only to reappear at another place, and to rise resurrected in a new and more brilliant garb. They may change their names and even their meaning, according to the emphasis laid upon one or other of their aspects, without losing their original direction: because it is in the nature of a symbol to be as manifold as the life from which it grew, and yet to retain its character, its organic unity within the diversity of all aspects."*
>
> Foundations of Tibetan Mysticism
> Lama Anagarika Govinda

Ancient Mudras & Yantras

In India's primitive religions, rites played an important role in expressing the mystical character of their spirituality. Dance, as an integral part of the rite, abounded with choreographic hand-gestures which brought out magical and ritualistic components. Over time these original dance gestures underwent many changes in form and meaning. Assuming greater religious significance, they were further incorporated into various spiritual traditions and adapted to fit their unique metaphysical symbolism.

Ritualistic use of sacred hand-gestures or 'mudras' has found a particularly lively expression in Tantric practices of India and Tibet. In Buddhist Tantra the mudra, the mantra and the inner attitude were blended into the ritual, facilitating the experience of Oneness. This state beyond male-female polar opposites is referred to as Mahamudra or Great Attitude, giving its name to one of the most important meditation systems in Tibet.[23]

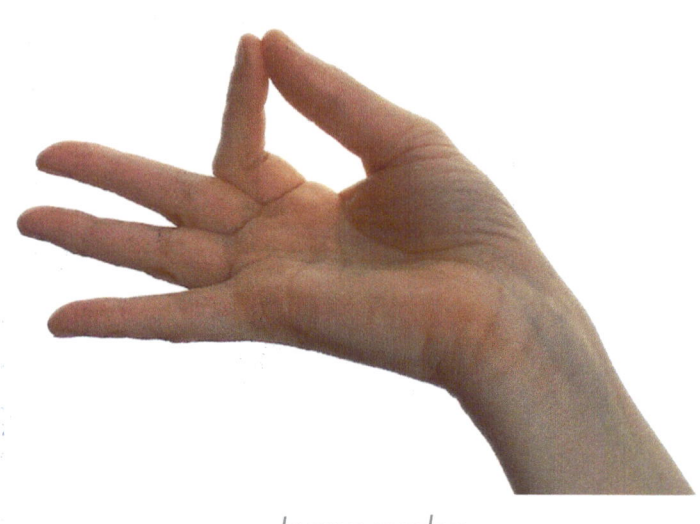
Jnana-mudra

The Sanskrit word 'mudra' means a seal or a sign, indicating that it was used to seal and enforce the effectiveness of religious rituals, or as a sign to identify specific deities and esoteric truths. Mudras were implemented in a variety of ways: a) as transcendental symbols of universal truths, b) to invoke and worship deities in religious ceremonies, c) to induce spiritual trance states, d) as power yoga and meditation tools aimed at controlling and channeling subtle energies and e) for healing. In the rich spiritual heritage abounding with hundreds of hand gestures, Abhaya-mudra ('the gesture of fearlessness') and Dhyana-mudra ('the meditation gesture') are most commonly used in the Buddhist tradition. In Hindu Tantrism, 'Jnana-mudra' ('the wisdom seal') is the most popular meditation gesture.[24]

Yantras are known as sacred power diagrams utilized for ritual and meditation purposes.[25] The Sanskrit word 'yantra' means an instrument or device for concentration and visualization. It is a geometric structure, shaped out of simple, elementary forms such as the dot, circle, square and triangle. These primary shapes were combined with almost mathematical precision into an inexhaustible variety of abstract geometric designs. Each shape assumed a variety of meanings depending on how it was used within the context of the total symbol.

3. If the Hands Could Talk

The symbology of yantra revolves around the 'bindu' or dot drawn into the center of its design. This is considered yantra's most fundamental aspect, conveying the cosmic truth of creation as a unified whole. It symbolizes the inherent unity of polarities, and on a personal level, the psychic wholeness of the individual. The perfection of geometric patterns alludes to the cosmic order that we encounter throughout all creation.

Used as a visual aid in meditation, yantras help to control mental fluctuations by gathering the mind into a single point at the center. Being archetypal symbols of wholeness, yantras also have a therapeutic value. Deep internalization of their geometric design during meditation, serves as a catalyst for healing the psychic split within the individual. The profound realization of Oneness conveyed through yantra's symbology coincides with the attainment of inner harmony and wholeness.

Shri Yantra

Yantras are drawn on flat surfaces such as silk, paper and wood, or engraved in gold, copper and rock crystal. The most famous is the Shri Yantra.[26] It encompasses the entire universe within its geometric structure and depicts the story of creation through various stages of cosmic evolution. More complex designs are called 'mandalas'.

Virtual Holo-Symbol

HOLO-SYMBOL

... is a koan, mind is the disciple.

... is a voiceless harp in the orchestra of light.

... is a sacred seal that burns holes in the veil of maya.

... is the pointer to the surreal spectacle of optical illusion.

... is a geometric apparition that seduces the mind into meditation.

... is a cosmic grinder pulverizing solid pieces into the fine dust of pure awareness.

... is a signpost at the four-dimensional crossroad in the time-space continuum.

... is a cosmic microscope into the quantum soup of matter.

... is a light prism converting colors back into white light.

... is mental gauze that sifts out impurities in the mind.

... is the mouth of the sage under the vow of silence.

... is a kaleidoscopic pacifier to the infant mind.

... is a hieroglyph of the Absolute.

3. If the Hands Could Talk

> THE HM SYMBOL IS 'A CROSS BETWEEN A MUDRA AND
> A YANTRA - WITH A HOLOGRAPHIC SPIN'.

If we compare HM symbols with ancient mudras or yantras, we notice many similarities. They are created with hands and embody universal principles - similar to mudras. They are used as geometric meditation devices - similar to yantras. From that point of view they all share a universal connection.

On the other hand, there are many structural differences between them. By comparison with ancient mudras, HM symbols are completely new shapes with stronger emphasis on the perfection of geometric symmetry. Unlike many single-handed mudras, the hands are united as a rule into one pattern in order to make a symbol of wholeness. By comparison with two-dimensional, static yantras, they are kinetic, 'holographically' enhanced symbols. HM symbols are dramatically altered when viewed in holomode. They become *holo-symbols*.

The relationship between the hand-symbol and the holo-symbol is that of positive and negative polarity, or the male and the female counterpart of the total symbol which they embody. The hand-symbol represents the female aspect because of its predominantly physical character. The holo-symbol is the male polarity because of its 'holographically' enhanced, transcendental character. Together they represent the totality of the symbol's meaning.

During transition from one shape to another, the hands come to 'talk'. They unfold a 'secret' by 'telling a story' in a wordless language. For example, the hand-symbol of Non-harming features an arrow pointing outwards. During transformation into a holo-symbol a reverse arrow appears pointing inwards, implying that aggression is essentially a self-destructive act.

The Path

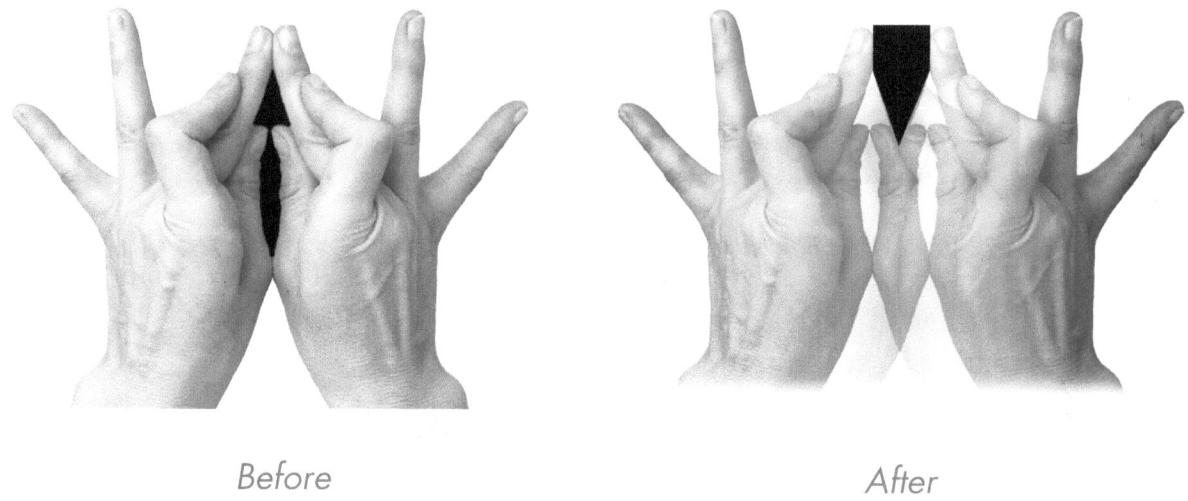

Before   *After*

Each one of the 12 symbols reveals hidden messages pertaining to its symbolic meaning, which are unavailable at first sight. It's only through meditation that we learn and understand the language of 'talking' symbols. *(see The Twelve Elixirs)*

These unique features distinguish Holographic Mudra Meditation from all existing symbolic systems.

The Alchemy of the Hands

When expansive esoteric concepts are 'compressed' into intelligible external forms, spiritual symbols are born. Examples are the Cross, the Yin-Yang, the Star of David, Shri Yantra and many other spiritual symbols which have been around for thousands of years. Under the 'umbrella' of the symbol, a vast amount of complex metaphysical information is contained which could not be expressed by means of ordinary

3. If the Hands Could Talk

language.

Because of their complexity, the 12 principles of Unified Awareness are systematically presented, making Holographic Mudra Meditation into a coherent symbolic system. They are made by interlacing the fingers of both hands into symmetrical geometric designs. The fingers are symbolic channels of action through which mental energies flow. Their unique synergy creates an 'energetic seal' which has a harmonizing effect on the mind.

THUMB (*Earth Element / Taurus Line*)

~ the principle of matter ~

The thumb symbolizes body awareness as the densest form of the ego-complex. Emerging from the root of the hand and the Venus mound, it is linked to the sensation function and the Earth element: out of sensual love, the physical body is born. Lowest in height compared to other fingers, it represents the platform below, the solid foundation providing firm hold for all other fingers.

FOREFINGER (*Air Element / Jupiter Line*)

~ the principle of creative expression and higher knowledge ~

The forefinger is associated with the Air element and the higher thinking function called the Divine Mind or Higher Self. The emphasis is on inspired wisdom which extends beyond the personal into the social arena, thus benefiting the whole. It is with our minds that we co-create the world around us. Thus the principle of creative expression is embedded in the prolific creativity of the mind.

MIDDLE FINGER *(Ether Element / Saturn Line)*
~ the principle of Universal Law ~

The middle finger symbolizes the Ether element and the principle of Universal Law. It alludes to the highest spiritual superstructure or the cosmic order which underlies and governs the manifest universe - called Dharma in Buddhism or Hinduism.

RING FINGER *(Fire Element / Sun Line)*
~ the principle of individuation ~

The ring finger is associated with personal identity or self-consciousness. It represents the Fire element and the function of intuition. It symbolizes the journey of the hero in his quest for self-realization which in Jungian terms is the process of individuation. Here one is called to purposeful action (Fire) and endeavors to fulfill his special destiny and purpose in life.

LITTLE FINGER *(Water Element / Mercury Line)*
~ the principle of intellect ~

The little finger symbolizes the human mind or the intellect which focuses more on detail rather than the whole. It operates through analysis, dividing, fragmenting and comparing information and perceptions as a method of understanding. It is associated with the Water element because our thinking is often subjective and emotionally colored.

3. If the Hands Could Talk

The geometric pattern represents the meaning contained within the symbol. Our visual identification with the external shape corresponds to its internal content. The physical symbol is the energetic portal or doorway into the symbol's content. Through this reciprocal relationship of inside and outside, form and content, gross and subtle, the seed of awareness within is activated.

The Common Ground

HM symbols differ from one another in external shape and symbolic meaning. At the same time they share similar characteristics as representations of the following values: pattern, movement, symmetry, center and oneness.

PATTERN

At the subatomic level, all particles in solid materials are arranged and interlocked into clear, definite patterns. As symmetrical geometric shapes, HM symbols convey the notion that everything in the manifest universe is an expression of energy vibrating in a multitude of wave patterns, including our thoughts and ideas.

MOVEMENT

Besides their static, physical shape, HM symbols display a kinetic aspect during Hologazing meditation. They become 'alive' in front of the gazing eyes, going back and forth between solid and transparent mode. Resembling fluid, vibrating holograms of light, these symbols expand beyond their material form to illuminate the intangible.

Observing this dynamic interplay between form and formlessness has a liquefying, dissolving effect on our deeply ingrained, rigid concepts about the solidity of matter.

SYMMETRY

Something is considered symmetrical if it has one dividing axis or more, looking the same from different angles. A mirror reflection of two identical halves is the type of symmetry most commonly found in nature and living organisms. For example, each particle has a symmetrical antiparticle with an equal mass but an opposite charge. The human body is a perfect example of 'reflection symmetry'.[27] Divided by an axis, the hands tied into an HM symbol are perfect mirrors of each other. Meditation on them instills a sense of equilibrium within.

CENTER

HM symbols are geometric whirlpools with a magnetic center. While meditating on them our mind circles around the seed idea until it penetrates the symbol's inner core. At that point we comprehend its meaning at the innermost level. This meditation leads to a transmutation of mental clutter until the golden seed of insight is revealed from within. The harvest can only be reaped when the distracted mind is harnessed in one-pointed meditation.

ONENESS

The human brain is divided into two hemispheres which are connected at the center through a nerve bundle called the 'corpus collosum'.[26] The left brain is more rational and analytical and controls the right side of the body, while the right is more irrational and intuitive, controlling the left side. Bringing both hands together and aligning them in perfectly symmetrical shapes corresponds to the alignment between our left and right visual fields. There are physical neural connections which run between the eyes and the two sides of the brain. Therefore, the act of creating a hand-

3. If the Hands Could Talk

symbol naturally establishes balance between the left and right hemispheres and helps reconnect their circuitry.

According to the scientific split-brain studies, we have two autonomous minds, each associated with one hemisphere. Both are co-conscious, feeling what the other side experiences through their neural connections. In order to be healthy it is important to balance any extreme dominance of the left or the right brain, and establish a constructive relationship between two minds.[29] Embodying a marriage of the male-female polarity, these hand-symbols invoke a state of perfect union within. Creating a bridge between the hands signifies the merging of our dual aspects. Regular practice is conducive to mental health as well as the realization of Oneness.

The goal of meditating on the symbols is to:
1. *develop concentration*
2. *gain deeper understanding of the symbol's meaning*
3. *integrate that understanding into practical life*

Taming the Monkey Mind

CONCENTRATION: No matter what activity we perform, it requires our attention. But the mind has a tendency to slip away and be distracted. This habitual mode of mental wandering is not easy to counter. For most people it is difficult to bring the mind back again and again to a desired task. Like the wind, it's hard to control and prevent it from dissipating in many different directions.

Such a state of mind is often referred to as mental agitation or excessive stirring of the mind. It is characterized by thoughts randomly jumping from one subject to another, just as a monkey leaps from branch to branch. When the mind is agitated, it is very difficult to perform at peak level. When we let our scattered thoughts sidetrack us from one inconsequential activity to another, a waste of time and effort is unavoidable. In the long run, unused talents, lost opportunities and many disappointments in life could have been avoided by simply learning to better focus our mind. In order to increase our effectiveness and performance levels in life, it is necessary to amplify our mental power by developing laser-like concentration.

Although there are many different meditation styles and techniques for the development of concentration, the underlying principle is always the same: *one-pointedness*. One meditates on the breath, a sound or a visual object, in order to focus the mind and offset mental distractions. For example, when practicing pranayama ('breath control' in Sanskrit), full attention is paid to the subtle process of inhalation and exhalation. Closely observing the rhythmical flow of air in and out of the lungs has a centering effect on the mind, which helps develop concentration.

During an HM meditation session, the mind is guided through several progressive stages of concentration. The first step is the creation of the hand-symbol, which can be challenging because we haven't yet developed a sense of coordination between the fingers. Strong emphasis on geometric symmetry necessitates our undivided attention, the first step in developing concentration. As though we are building an architectural construct with our hands, we must approach it with patience and great precision. With practice we master the creation of the symbol so that both hands snap into perfect alignment and any initial discomfort falls away. With each symbol we discover a pleasant, comforting sensation in our hands, caused by the energies flowing harmoniously through the energetic seal.

The next step of concentration involves Hologazing, causing the physical hand-symbol to become a kinetic holo-symbol. Our hands become a 'holoidoscope', a kaleidoscopic device which we hold to our eye and watch the formation of unusual symmetrical patterns appearing out of thin air. It can be compared to an etheric exercise

3. If the Hands Could Talk

machine designed for flexing and strengthening the mind's muscles.

The visual effects are mysterious and quite appealing, effortlessly engaging and focusing the mind. The element of surprise and newness caused by the slightest movement of the fingers entices the mind to stay on course, following closely in the steps of ever-changing geometric forms. Because of their fluid character, nothing is forced or artificial about these meditation exercises. The shapes move in a very subtle and highly structured fashion because of their geometric nature. These dynamics provide a perfect tool for the development of concentration, making HM symbols very effective meditation instruments.

In the final stage of concentration exercise, what was our initial focus on the external form of the symbol progresses towards an even finer realm. With our eyes closed, we visualize the geometric pattern of the holo-symbol on our mental screen and link it to its abstract symbolic meaning.

In this journey from creation of the hand-symbol to its re-creation as a mental blueprint, we have progressed from the gross to the more subtle stage of the symbol. Regular practice of all these steps gradually equips the mind with greater powers of concentration, and automatically reflects in better performance in our daily life. Also this practice is necessary as preparation for next stage of meditation.

Shaking the Tree of Knowledge

MEDITATION: The 12 symbols represent the key concepts which play an important role in our lives. Their understanding is fundamental to the shaping of our worldview and structuring our existence and in order to refine our understanding we must inquire beyond the intellect delving more deeply into their essence. Because of their complexity and abstract nature, we must meditate deeply about them before we can apply our insights in practical life.

Every idea exists as a specific vibratory pattern within our energy body. When we are talking about the 12 symbols, we are essentially talking about them as frequencies of universal magnitude. Meditating on the symbol's meaning with a concentrated mental force is like shining a flashlight into the vast storehouse of Spirit. We are searching in the unknown until we find an angle which illuminates the vibratory pattern of the idea - Love, for example. As soon as we tap into the code of the symbol's vibration, our knowledge about it becomes activated.

In other words, when we finally attune our mind to the frequency of Love, it begins to pulsate through our whole being. Our mind is like radar, sending signals or rippling waves through our total energy field. When we say we feel love, it means that we are feeling those pleasant vibrations pulsing through us. And when we totally assimilate and synchronize our energy body with those frequencies, we experience a profound breakthrough in our understanding. Merging with those frequencies coincides with our knowing the true meaning of love or any other concept we are meditating on. Because it came from within, such knowledge is far more accurate and personal in comparison to limited definitions based more on external information. That is why meditation always guides our quest for knowledge - *inside*.

Even though our thoughts are intangible they represent very powerful, subtle vibratory frequencies. A thought is like a chord struck on the instrument of our mind,

3. If the Hands Could Talk

resonating for a while through our energy field. When we begin our meditation on a symbol, for example Love, our goal is to quiet all other thoughts down so that our chosen idea can come to the foreground. If our mind is in a state of confusion, vibrational frequencies of many different thoughts collide with and distort the frequency pattern of our main theme. All incompatible frequencies cancel each other out. For example, any fearful thoughts intersecting our meditation will destabilize the vibrational frequency of love which we are trying to attune to. If our mind is jumping from one frequency of thought to another, it becomes impossible to maintain the same frequency of love during meditation. It's like playing several songs at the same time; the mixture of sounds results in discordant noise which disharmonizes our body-mind. Being able to keep our focus steady is essential in the process of meditation. In that sense, meditation is essentially a very simple and effortless affair. There is nothing really difficult about it, except for being able internally to play the same 'song' for a while, until we learn the lyrics.

Reaping the Fruits

INTEGRATION: Our knowledge is subject to memory loss and unless we bring it into conscious awareness again and again, it dissolves into the oblivion of the unconscious. We simply forget. We close out the 'documents' and file them away. True spiritual knowledge is not something we switch on and off. We truly 'know' something if we can practice whenever necessary. For example, purely intellectual understanding of Non-harming is essentially useless unless we are able to apply it whenever the occasion dictates.

It takes sustained, conscious effort to reprogram deeply-engrained habitual behavior, even if it's just biting your nails. The 12 symbols help us isolate specific problem areas in our life and then systematically to work toward improving them. For example, if our problem is addiction, we practice Self-mastery meditation. If we are in survival mode and plagued by anxiety or financial problems, we focus on the Prosperity meditation. If we are prone to anger, arguments or violence, then we turn to Non-harming meditation.

Each of the 12 meditations has a specific purpose, offering very concrete steps toward self-improvement. If we are honest with ourselves and truly dedicated to our personal growth, we'll be able to easily see our progress in everyday situations. For instance, if we have been practicing Non-harming we'll become highly conscious of whether or not our actions in any way conflict with this principle. At the point of mastery we can no longer be provoked into angry or violent behavior. This level of achievement is a sure sign that we are making true spiritual progress and reaping the fruits of our efforts.

Every time we bring our hands together in a hand-symbol we create a 'bead of awareness'. It becomes a reminder, a signpost on the crossroads of life, guiding us in the right direction. Through constant repetition we continue infusing this awareness deeper into our core levels until it becomes a more permanent state of mind. The process of reprogramming our mind is like stringing these beads on the necklace of time, till we fill in all the gaps in the time-space continuum.

Prototype Meditation Sequence

To get the full benefit, both mini-sessions as well as full sessions should be incorporated into the HM meditation program. A mini-session consists of creating the hand-symbol and then Hologazing for a couple of minutes, as often as possible during the day. What follows is the instruction of how to practice the longer, full meditation sequence.

3. If the Hands Could Talk

Posture: (see page 44)

Breathing: In preparation for a full session, do the following breathing routine to calm the mind and clear it from mental clutter.

Begin with *alternate nostril breathing*. (One inhalation-exhalation counts as 1 cycle.) Start with four cycles of breathing through one nostril and then repeat them through the other nostril. Always close your nostril with the thumb of the corresponding hand, with all other fingers pointing straight up. The breathing should be energetic and fast. Go back and forth between the left and right nostrils eight times.

In the finishing phase take a long, deep inhalation through both nostrils. Hold the breath as long as you can and then exhale slowly through both nostrils. Finally, return to normal breathing and relax. (3-5 min.)

Concentration: Bring the hands together and create the hand-symbol according to the instructions. (*See The Twelve Elixirs*) Make sure that geometric symmetry is achieved and that the hand-posture is comfortable. Now lift your arms in the air and position the hand-symbol approximately ten inches in front of your eyes. As you Hologaze observe the original, physical shape change into fluid 'holographic' imagery. After several minutes, release the hands and place them comfortably on your lap. Now close your eyes and straighten and relax your back. Visualize the exact shape of the holo-symbol internally, on your mental screen. Link the geometric shape with its symbolic meaning. (5 min.)

Meditation: With your eyes closed, direct your attention towards the abstract meaning of the symbol. If you become distracted by other thoughts, bring your awareness back to the main theme by silently repeating the name of the symbol, like a positive affirmation. The meaning is like a koan, a riddle for awakening the mind. In this process of introspection illuminating thoughts and ideas will start surfacing. Observe them closely, refining and crystallizing your understanding of the symbol. In the final stage of the meditation session, let go of all thoughts until your mind is brought to a point of perfect stillness. In this deep, effortless state, you will find yourself tuned in to the vibrational frequency of the symbol, attaining a "knowing" beyond all thought.

The duration of the full session should vary from half an hour up to a full hour and should be practiced 2-3 times a week (or more if desired), in combination with daily mini-sessions.

The Twelve Elixirs

1. How Do I Think?

The Twelve Elixirs

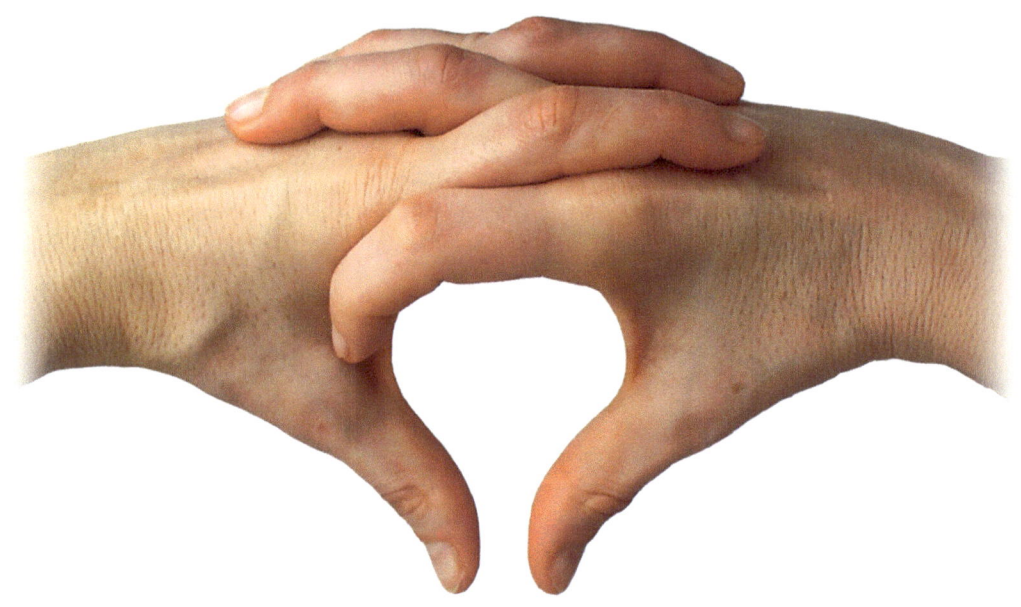

The Hand-symbol of Spirit

1. How Do I Think?

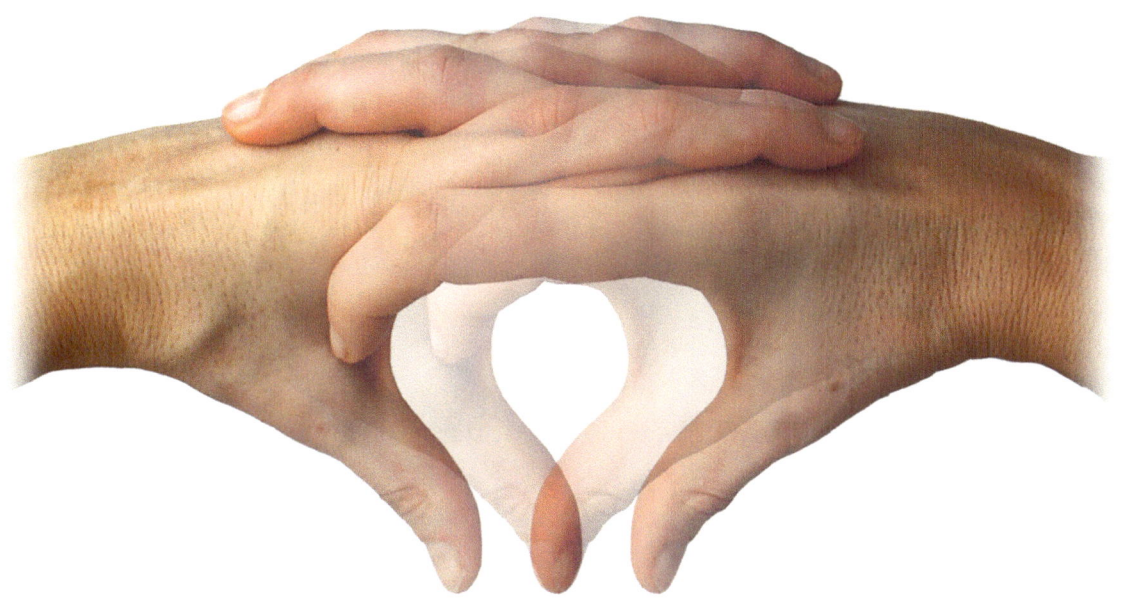

The Holo-symbol of Spirit

Spirit

[THE UNIVERSAL WOMB]

The hand-symbol of Spirit embodies the primordial womb, the cosmic pro-creatrix giving birth to Creation. The thumbs represent the positive and the negative poles of Nature. Hologazing through the point between the thumbs results in a visual effect: a virtual 'drop of matter' condensing before our eyes from no tangible source. Thus the holo-symbol plays out the mystery of genesis by simulating the very act of creation at the most primal level: 'creatio ex nihilo', the proverbial egg dropping into the tangible realm out of empty space. Just as the holographic model of the universe suggests, through interference or criss-crossing of polarities, the creation 'fertilizes itself' into physical manifestation.

Looking at the purposeful complexity and beauty of life, it becomes quite obvious that it was created not by chance but according to an unlimited, intelligent design. Spirit is the absolute creative force in the universe, whose nature is the quintessential act of creation. Creative Intelligence is the ultimate common denominator of all Creation.

Seeing the universality of the Spirit as the creative principle behind everything has a unifying effect on all people, in spite of their religious, philosophical or ethnic differences. Spirit meditation deepens and enriches our life within the spiritual dimension. It promotes a universal orientation which doesn't lead to conflict and separation based on external differences.

Spirit meditation is recommended for:
Developing a universal spiritual orientation, transcending our differences, deepening a relationship with the Divine.

1. How Do I Think?

TECHNIQUE:

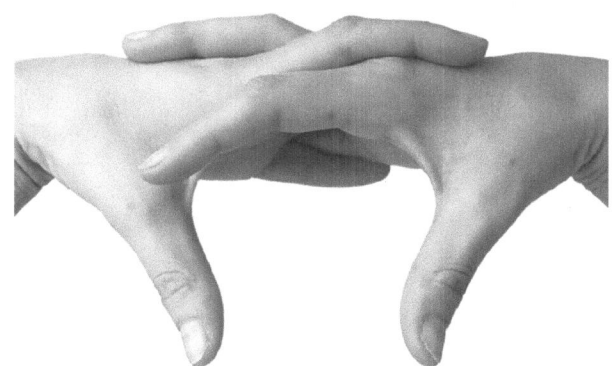

1. Interlace all the fingers (except the thumbs).

2. Bring the thumbs closer together (approx. $1/3$ inch apart), pointing downwards.

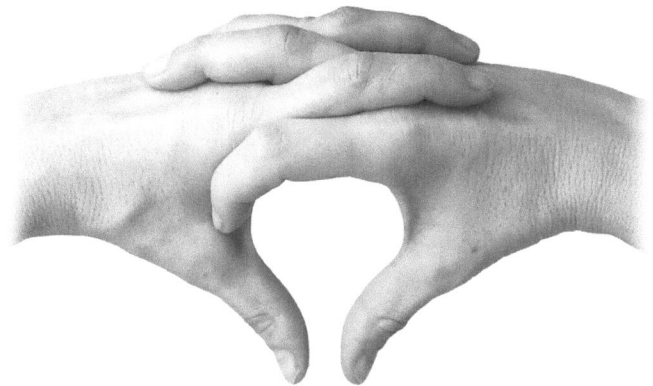

The Twelve Elixirs

The Hand-symbol of Matter

1. How Do I Think?

The Holo-symbol of Matter

Matter

[THE WEB]

The hand-symbol of Matter is a geometric representation of the spiritual in the physical dimension. The material order is symbolically captured in a diamond shape whose four cardinal points allude to the four directions: East, West, North and South. Inside it, four smaller diamond shapes are contained, symbolizing the primary elements of creation: Earth, Water, Fire and Air. The whole geometric arrangement resembles a web-like image, revolving around the center point where the diagonals cross. This dot in the middle symbolizes the Ether element within which all other elements are contained. It represents the single principle of Spirit from which the web-like, vibratory currents expand and contract.

In Hindu cosmology, "there is the metaphor of a spider sitting at the centre of its web, issuing and reabsorbing its threads in concentric circles, all held at one point. [...] The metaphor also alludes to the Indian vision of the structure of the cosmos as a 'holon', growing and expanding in concentric circles, and then contracting, dissolving into a single principle."[30]

Imitating this archetypal model of creation, the hand-symbol of Matter makes a kinetic shift into the holo-symbol whereby the original shapes are recomposed, radiating from the center in a concentric manner. Despite the polarization and the changes which occur, the whole as a closed structure remains in an irrevocable state of perfect balance. Each side complements the other and they are held together at the center. The new geometric arrangement is created by the simultaneous contrasting of patterns, just like the vibratory wave patterns that we encounter at the subatomic level.

1. How Do I Think?

This meditation exercise softens our rigid perception of the solidity of matter, which continually reinforces separation and materialistic tendencies in us. It reminds us that the material world is essentially made up of wave patterns which have become permanently interlocked, giving matter its solid appearance.

Matter meditation is recommended for:

Overcoming extreme materialism, attachments to material possessions and worldly desires.

The Twelve Elixirs

TECHNIQUE:

1. Form the Saturn fingers into an upward pointing triangle and the Sun fingers into a downward pointing triangle.

2. Join each Jupiter finger to its thumb and then put them together.

1. How Do I Think?

3. Hide the Mercury fingers behind the Sun fingers.

The Twelve Elixirs

The Hand-symbol of Oneness

1. How Do I Think?

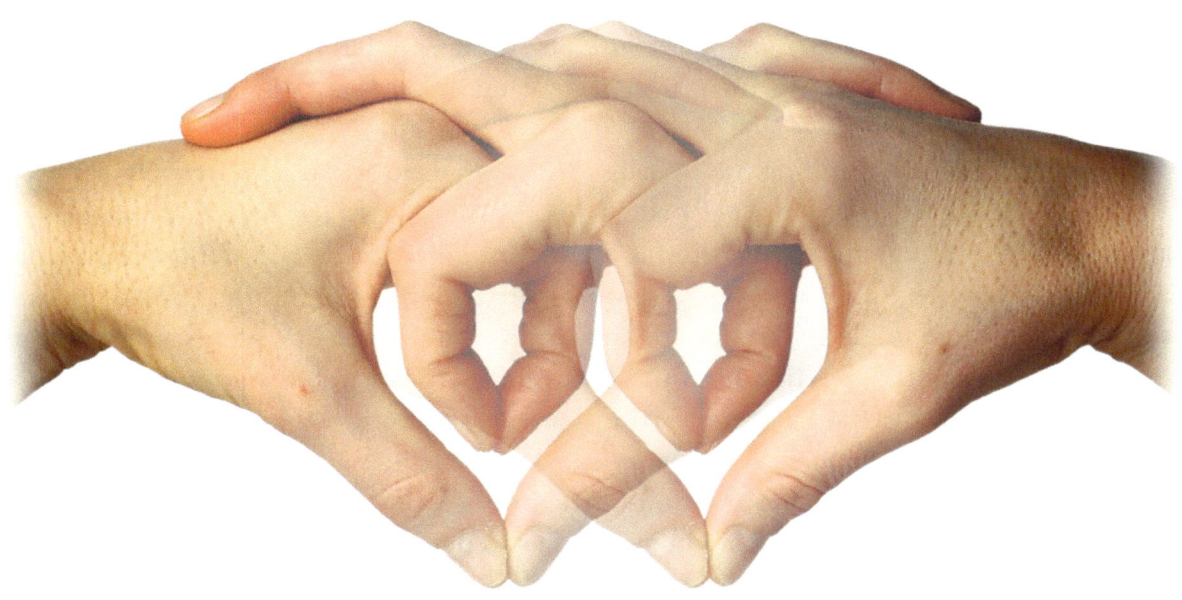

The Holo-symbol of Oneness

Oneness

[THE COSMIC EMBRACE]

This hand-symbol features a circle embraced by a larger circle, symbolizing the 'seed of creation' contained within the infinite body of Spirit. When it transforms into the holo-symbol, the inner circle doubles. This represents the primal division of unity, the original separation between Spirit and Matter. Even though the emerging forms are assuming seemingly separate identities, they remain in a state of unity, contained within the circle of Oneness.

In our dualistic thinking, we perceive Matter and Spirit as diametrically opposed and mutually exclusive because they stand for two seemingly irreconcilable aspects of reality. We see the physical dimension as the realm of multiplicity, where living beings and things exist separately in a tangible world. On the other hand, the spiritual world is an abstract, intangible realm beyond the reach of our ordinary senses. The crux of the paradox lies in the fact that both these extremes are essentially opposite ends of an infinite spectrum. Grasping the underlying sameness of both extremes has always been difficult and challenging for the human mind. And yet, the realization of their inherent unity is fundamental importance for a holistic outlook on life.

Meditation on the symbol of Oneness helps to deepen a feeling of universal closeness toward all peoples of the world. The goal is to attain a non-dual perception and release prejudices against others based on ethnic, national, cultural and other differences which lead to alienation, conflict and mutually destructive behavior.

Oneness meditation is recommended for:
Developing a non-dual perception, transcending our differences, deepening a feeling of closeness toward all living beings.

1. How Do I Think?

Technique:

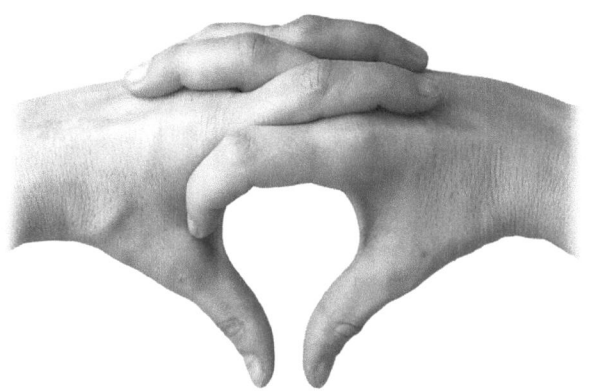

1. Interlace all fingers and connect the thumbs, pointing downwards.

2. Make a circle with the Jupiter fingers.

2. How Do I Act?

The Twelve Elixirs

The Hand-symbol of Compassion

2. How Do I Act?

The Holo-symbol of Compassion

Compassion

[THE CROSS]

When we have achieved Oneness, compassion becomes a natural virtue. Our personal heart expands into an all-embracing cosmic heart, beating for all living beings. The hand-symbol of Compassion resembles a heart shape with an inscribed cross, symbolizing the crossroads - a place where individual and collective interests meet. When the hand-symbol transforms into the holo-symbol a circle emerges in the center of a criss-crossing pattern, alluding to the unity between personal ambition and collective interest. Out of compassion, we sacrifice selfish personal goals if they are of disservice to the whole.

Compassion is a highly developed sensitivity towards others, particularly their pain and suffering. Concern for the wellbeing of all people awakens in us altruistic motivations. The greater our identification with the world, the stronger the desire to act for the benefit of the whole. We consciously choose not to benefit singly by exploiting or destroying any part of creation. We cannot live in isolation or be concerned only with personal agendas lest we reap the negative karma of collective neglect. Sooner or later a separatist attitude towards life comes back to haunt us personally, in the form of wars, pollution, or crime. Benevolent action on behalf of all automatically benefits the individual, as we are all an inseparable part of the whole.

This meditation helps us to realize compassion within ourselves. It deepens an awareness of belonging to the global community and awakens in us a 'team spirit'.

Compassion meditation is recommended for:
Awakening compassion and humanitarian aspirations, transmuting greed, selfishness and egoism.

2. How Do I Act?

TECHNIQUE:

1. Connect the thumbs, the Jupiter and the Mercury fingers at their tips.

2. Interlace the Saturn and the Sun fingers.

The Twelve Elixirs

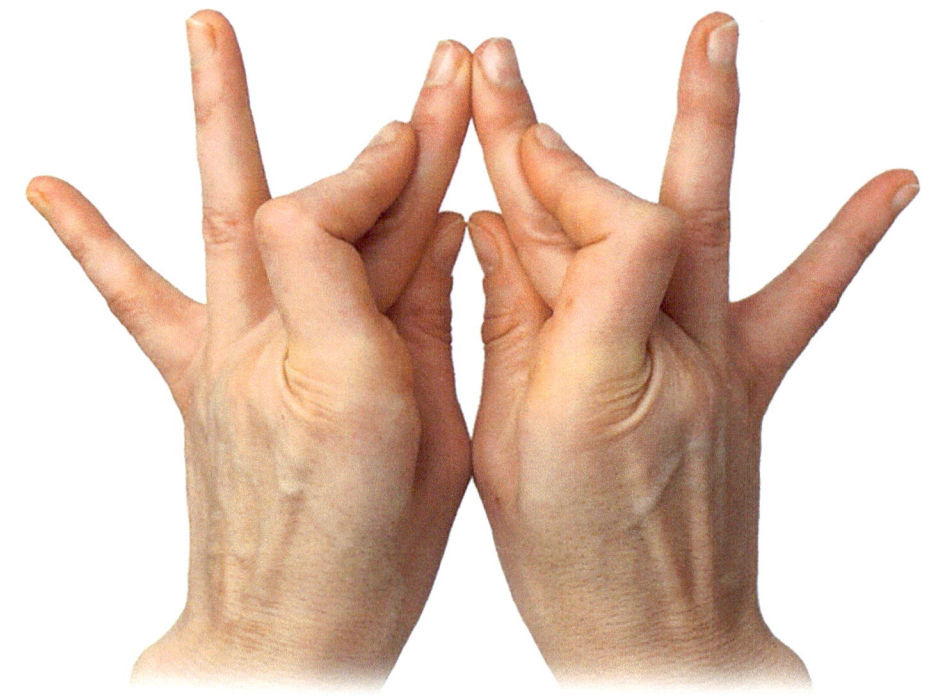

The Hand-symbol of Non-harming

2. How Do I Act?

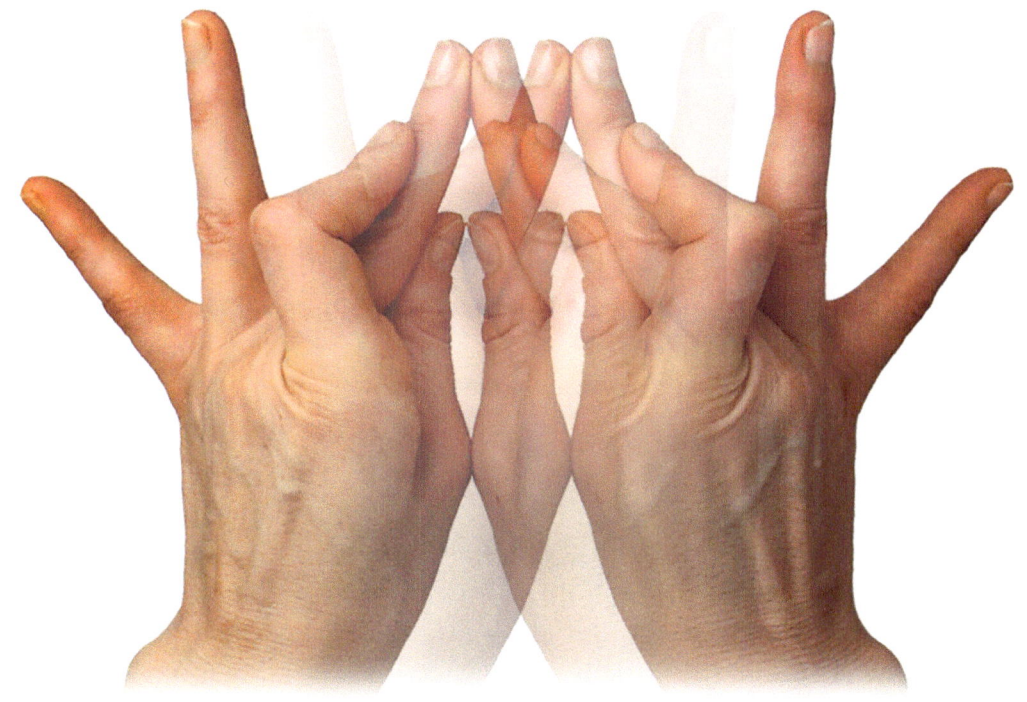

The Holo-symbol of Non-harming

Non-harming

[THE ARROW BOOMERANG]

This hand-symbol resembles a weapon with sharp edges. In the center we see the outline of an arrow pointing outward, symbolizing an aggressive attitude and the destructive power that comes with it.

When the hand-symbol shifts into the holo-symbol, a reverse action of the arrow can be observed: an inward pointing arrow emerges, cutting like a knife into our own flesh. Just as the saying 'what goes around, comes around' implies, the individual becomes the receiver of his or her own aggression.

When we have achieved Oneness every act of aggression becomes a self-destructive act which is, of course, unnatural. As we develop a more inclusive relationship with all living beings and the environment as an expanded part of ourselves, aggressive behavior 'falls off' as an evolutionary waste product.

In situations where conflict arises, the right thing to do is disengage. This makes the difference between spiritually correct and spiritually incorrect action. Honoring all life to the highest degree, monks often retreated to an isolated environment such as a monastery in order to avoid even the slightest involvement and exposure to violence. While such a lifestyle may not be appropriate for everyone, it is still the responsibility of us all to heighten our awareness and make intelligent choices which do not lead to aggression. Much of human suffering is self-created and could be avoided through conscious prevention and self-control. Non-harming is the art of peaceful coexistence. Regular practice of this meditation helps to remold our aggressive behavior patterns.

Non-harming meditation is recommended for:
Reprogramming anger or aggressive behavior patterns, developing self-control.

2. How Do I Act?

TECHNIQUE:

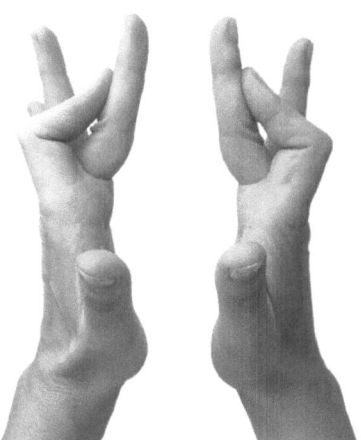

1. Place the Jupiter fingers on top of the Saturn fingers and pull Jupiter slightly backwards.

2. Facing each other, connect the length of both thumbs.

3. Join the Saturn fingers, creating an arrow in the middle. The Sun and the Mercury fingers will be pointing outwards.

The Twelve Elixirs

The Hand-symbol of Love

2. How Do I Act?

The Holo-symbol of Love

Love

[THE RING]

The symbol of Love resembles a heart shape divided into the left and right heart chambers, signifying the male and female polarity. When the hand-symbol becomes transformed into the holo-symbol, a circle or a ring - an archetypal symbol of wholeness - emerges at the center. It represents the liaison or the connecting link needed to bring the two halves together. It is the ring which marries the polarities into a unified whole. This ring is the symbol of love, the binding glue of relationships. Without the creative interplay, the weaving and the merging of energies through relationships, there is no alchemy, there is no creation. The ring also represents the heartwarming, all-embracing 'inner circle of love'.

The affection we feel towards each other naturally opens the door to greater ease and flexibility in relationships, enhancing our ability to share and cooperate. Love, the connective tissue, effortlessly brings us together. Usually, the closer the relationship, the greater our display of affection, and vice versa. However, when we become realized in Oneness we are able to unconditionally extend this affectionate attitude of loving kindness even further out into the world. Our loving radiance flows out to plants, animals and Mother Earth more abundantly. Despite the fact that we all are so different and often have little or nothing in common, we are able to fit the whole creation inside our 'inner circle'. How large or small, all-inclusive or exclusive, is your 'inner circle'?

Love meditation helps to refine our ability to communicate and relate to others more harmoniously. The mastery of love reflects in the generosity of heart and unconditional benevolence towards all.

Love meditation is recommended for:
Developing 'love consciouosness', letting go of hatred, improving relationships.

2. How Do I Act?

TECHNIQUE:

1. Connect all fingers at their tips, except for the Saturn fingers.

2. Place the Saturn fingers in the joint of the thumbs.

3. Connect the Saturn fingers back to back.

3. How Do I Feel?

The Twelve Elixirs

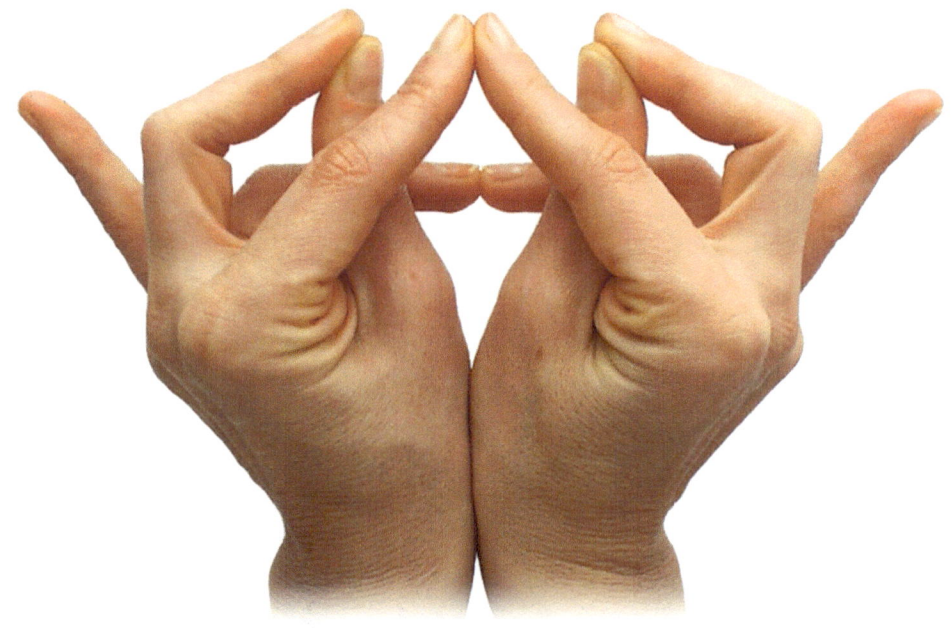

The Hand-symbol of Power

3. How Do I Feel?

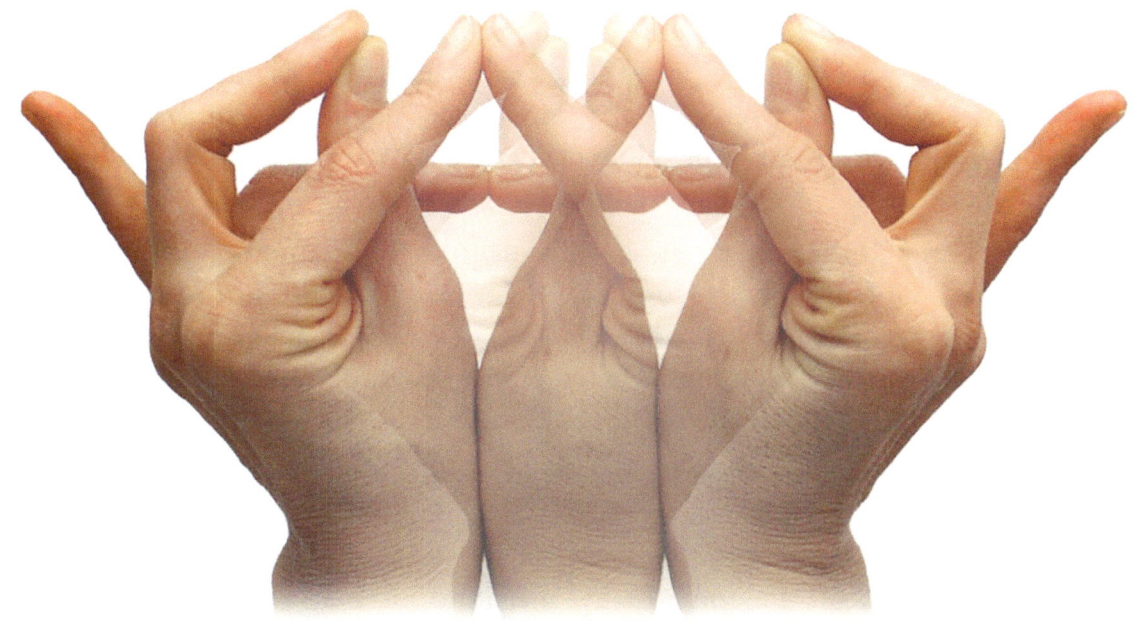

The Holo-symbol of Power

Power

[BEYOND THE VEIL]

This hand-symbol embodies the 'crown of enlightened awareness', granting insight beyond the veil of sensory perception. In the process of Hologazing, a virtual stripe shaped like an hourglass emerges vertically across the diamond in the center. Being in the foreground, it obscures the Sun fingers in the background. Despite its realness, we cannot be fooled by its solid appearance, just as we cannot be fooled by the solid appearance of the physical world in general.

Seeing through the veil of the senses leads to the profound realization that consciousness, and not matter, is the source of Creation. The 'Universal Mind' is the ultimate creative power. The concept of consciousness as the primary reality was embraced by many ancient spiritual traditions. The emerging scientific view is also accepting the idea that the world is actually the product of awareness.

All of us embody creative spiritual power. Personal power is an inner state of rousing creative potency which translates into a capacity to manifest desired realities. We exercise this power according to the degree of mental and creative energy at our disposal. To lift a rocket off the ground takes megatons of energy or power. In the same way, to accomplish our tasks and goals it takes a lot to make them a tangible reality. With greater mind power we can accomplish things faster and more effectively. Negativity, self-doubt, confusion, etc., are all energy leaks which can diminish our inner resources.

When we know what we want and consistently put forth concentrated energy, we can make things happen! The mind is a precision instrument, tailoring the fabric of

3. How Do I Feel?

life to fit our visions and desires. The more we are able to focus our mental powers, the easier it becomes. The purpose of this meditation is to strengthen the feeling of personal power by amplifying the creative potential of our mind.

Power meditation is recommended for:
Personal empowerment.

The Twelve Elixirs

TECHNIQUE:

1. Join the hands at the base of the thumbs. Connect the Jupiter fingers over the thumbs, pointing outwards.

2. Join the Saturn fingers with the thumbs.

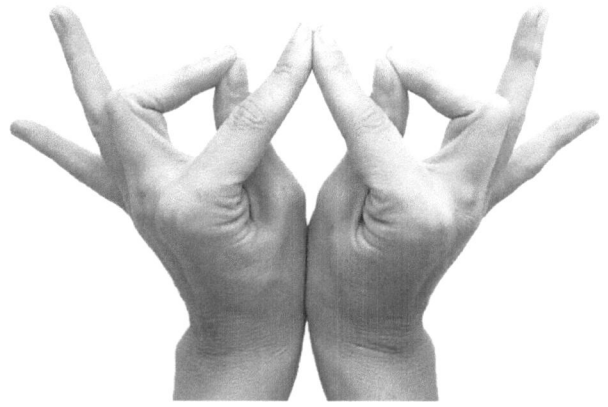

3. How Do I Feel?

3. Join the Sun fingers at the tips, creating a line.

The Twelve Elixirs

The Hand-symbol of Freedom

3. How Do I Feel?

The Holo-symbol of Freedom

Freedom

[THE LENS OF PERCEPTION]

Our mind is a lens of perception. We see the 'face of reality' through our individualized 'glasses', as represented by the hand-symbol of Freedom. We have a built-in mental filter through which we perceive and interpret reality. It skews our creative potential to fit into the narrow framework of our limited perception. For example, an unbalanced materialistic mentality can gear us toward the over-accumulation of material possessions.

Attainment of Freedom is closely related to the realization of our transcendental nature. Once we grasp it our perception changes and we are no longer so object-oriented. The realization that physical reality is not something set in stone has a liberating effect. Seeing consciousness and not matter as the primary reality shifts the emphasis toward the quality of relationships and the meaning we assign to things, rather than the things themselves. Such a fundamental change in perception dramatically alters our relationship with life, enabling us to 'reclaim our freedom'.

This is conveyed through the shift from the hand-symbol to a holo-symbol, whereby the original shape is transformed into a different pattern of greater transcendent quality. This alludes to the fact that the moment we shift our lens of perception we alter the total 'face of reality' - and accordingly our degree of freedom.

Seeing through the veil of our sensory perceptions helps temper the notion of solidity. As soon as we realize that reality is made out of sliding rather than fixed building blocks, participating in it with greater flexibility and creativity becomes more sensible. Then we are free to act upon and react to circumstances with a greater sense of

3. How Do I Feel?

detachment. We can choose them instead of being chosen by them. This new understanding enables us to move through life more gracefully and light-heartedly, without getting stuck in the rut of our rigid perceptions.

Freedom is an inner state of mind reflected in external circumstances as well. Too many responsibilities, lack of free time, stress, and entanglement in these circumstances can be signs of an eroding feeling of freedom. This meditation facilitates the perceptual shift to reinstate that lost sense of freedom, both within and without.

Freedom meditation is recommended for:
Reaching a higher degree of freedom in life.

TECHNIQUE:

1. Create a triangle with the Jupiter fingers and the thumbs.

2. Cross the Saturn fingers and place them on the thumbs.

3. How Do I Feel?

3. Connect the Sun fingers, pointing downwards. The Mercury fingers must be parallel with the Sun fingers.

The Twelve Elixirs

The Hand-symbol of Wholeness

3. How Do I Feel?

The Holo-symbol of Wholeness

Wholeness

[MANDALA OF THE SELF]

The hand-symbol of Wholeness embodies the 'mandala of the Self'. It resembles a geometric pattern with the left and the right wing, symbolizing the male-female polarity within. A diamond within a larger diamond shape alludes to the small ego-self within a Higher Self. When it transforms into a holo-symbol, a more complex, meandering pattern emerges. The central aspect of the holo-symbol is the geometric alignment between the Mercury and the Saturn fingers, which resembles 2 parallel sinusoidal waves. This alludes to the state of harmony between the body and the mind - the essence of wholeness.

Loss of wholeness implies a negation of something that has become a part of our life but which we find it difficult to accept. It may be illness, death, failure or any other negative fact of life. It's what we call our 'dark side'. The loss of wholeness arises from the disparity between two opposing facets of our life: between who we are and who we would like to be; what we have and what we wish we had; between our ambitions and their realization. It represents a fundamental discrepancy between the given reality and the desired reality, the body-mind split. The abyss between two irreconcilable aspects of our life is a major source of unhappiness.

The first step toward wholeness is to embrace our dark side. Instead of turning our backs and running away from it, we must learn to accept it and approach it rather as an opportunity for personal growth. There is a valuable lesson in it and Nature is bringing it to our attention. The inner conflict is ultimately a crystallization of living in disharmony with natural principles. Our pain is the proper measure of how much we're out of balance. Although we see it as opposition to our wellbeing, suffering is

3. How Do I Feel?

essentially Nature's 'vaccine', a valuable catalyst for healing and perfecting ourselves.

Wholeness meditation promotes the merging of all conflicting aspects of our life into a unified whole. Accepting that *everything* is essential to life accelerates the healing process as well as reflects in our external circumstances.

Wholeness meditation is recommended for:
Physical and psychic healing, finding balance and inner peace.

TECHNIQUE:

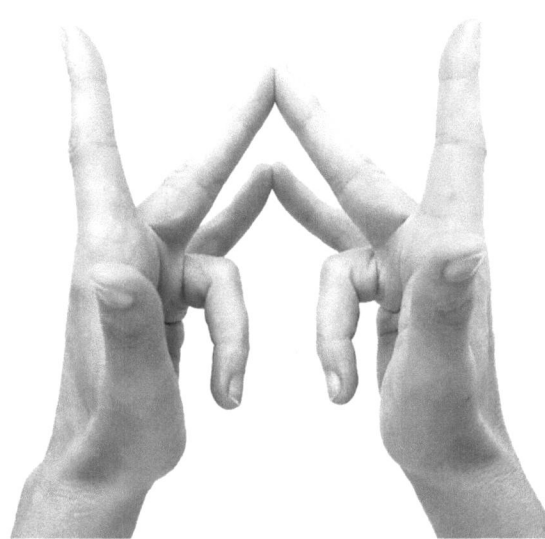

1. Connect the Saturn and the Mercury fingers at their tips. Drop and cross the Sun fingers.

2. Connect the base of the hands. The Sun fingers are to touch the base of the thumbs.

3. How Do I Feel?

3. Join the Jupiter fingers with the thumbs.

4. How Do I Materialize?

The Twelve Elixirs

The Hand-symbol of Prosperity

4. How Do I Materialize?

The Holo-symbol of Prosperity

Prosperity

[THE TREE OF LIFE]

The hand symbol of Prosperity is a branch-like image. The fingers are offshoots forking out from the main limbs, symbolic of the Tree of Life. When the hand symbol changes into the holo-symbol the fingers branch out further, representing new links in the chain of life. This is the main message of the symbol, reminding us that everything in Nature is made by linking its parts into myriad new combinations.

Nature is infinitely prolific. She thrives and prospers, eternally bearing her fruits. As part of nature we embody the same ability to create. Prosperity, in a broad sense, is an expression of our creative power on the material plane. It is the ability of the individual to be productive and prosper in life. Prosperity is not to be understood one-sidedly. Artistic creativity or any other pursuits which enrich our existence are all signs of prosperity and progress.

In a creative act our inner potential becomes manifest through external forms. When the flow of creative energy is blocked, we may experience scarcity and deprivation, or feel impoverished in life. Exuberant creativity and productivity can be seen as always bringing us prosperity.

This meditation exercise helps to stimulate the flow of our creative juices, increasing our productivity and prosperity.

Prosperity meditation is recommended for:

Healing existential anxiety, attracting prosperity, opening the flow of creative expression.

4. How Do I Materialize?

TECHNIQUE:

1. Place the Jupiter fingers on top of Saturn fingers and slide them slightly backwards.

2. Connect the Sun fingers and the thumbs at the tips, and join them.

3. Connect the Saturn and the Mercury fingers at their tips.

The Twelve Elixirs

The Hand-symbol of Self-mastery

4. How Do I Materialize?

The Holo-symbol of Self-mastery

Self-mastery

[THE KARMIC KNOT]

An overly materialistic worldview continually reinforces materialistic tendencies. Through overindulgence they can crystallize into addictions and compulsive behavior. Whenever we go to extremes Nature automatically presents us with an antidote, a corresponding karmic situation which urges us to regain balance in accordance with the Universal Law. However, deeply ingrained behavior patterns are very difficult to overcome. They harden into a 'karmic knot'.

In the symbol of Self-mastery, the Saturn fingers represent the principle of the Universal Law. They are knotted tightly, symbolizing the karmic knot which holds us back on our life path. Our lesson is to find the way out of such limitation. When the hand-symbol changes into the holo-symbol, the solution presents itself. As soon as we apply Hologazing, the knot opens up, assuming the shape of a keyhole with a dot in the middle. The dot symbolizes the key which opens the door to our destiny and personal growth. Being in the center, it alludes to the principle of 'at-one-ment' with universe. Living in harmony with Nature's principles is a precondition for the release from karmic blocks.

This meditation exercise promotes the awareness of living in harmony with Nature's Laws as a way of freeing ourselves from enslavement by bodily appetites and lower self.

Self-mastery meditation is recommended for:
Overcoming karmic blocks, mastering addictions, obsessions and compulsive behavior, strengthening will-power and self-discipline.

4. How Do I Materialize?

TECHNIQUE:

1. Join the thumbs and the Jupiter fingers.

2. Loop the Saturn fingers together. The Sun and the Mercury fingers are curled underneath.

The Twelve Elixirs

The Hand-symbol of Self-actualization

4. How Do I Materialize?

The Holo-symbol of Self-actualization

Self-actualization

[THE MYSTERY OF THE SEED]

Who am I? What is my purpose in life? These are universal questions which concern us all. Many of us are driven by an intrinsic desire to discover and express our unique identity. Our true nature is encoded in the seed of our DNA. In order to fulfill our life's purpose we must crack open that seed and unlock the mystery at its core. Only when the limited, ego-self merges with the Higher Self can the individual fulfill his highest destiny. Then our life's purpose extends beyond the personal realm and benefits the whole.

The hand symbol of Self-actualization portrays the seed within which our essence is enfolded. In the center of the hand-symbol the Saturn fingers are connected facing each other, signifying a closed unit, a seed holding the secret within. When the hand-symbol changes into a holo-symbol an upwardly-pointing arrow appears, penetrating the core of the seed. By cracking open the nutshell of the ego, we open the innermost chamber of our Higher Self, represented by Saturn fingers.

The process of Self-actualization can be compared to an archer shooting arrows at a target whose center symbolizes the true self. Although we may send out a lot of energy and enthusiasm, we don't always score a hit. Sometimes the arrow misses the target and disappears into the void. In other words, our endeavors fail to bring us the expected fulfillment. We have a sense of self-worth only to the degree that our actions reflect our true nature.

When we have a hard time realizing our goals in life it's generally because of the discrepancy between who we are deep down inside, and who we think we should be. We wear a mask in order to meet externally imposed standards. These superficial percep-

4. How Do I Materialize?

tions tend to lead us astray, alienating us from our true identity. They become a repelling force which pulls us away from our spiritual center, away from our core self.

The purpose of this meditation is to accelerate the process of self-discovery, and to gain insight into our true nature and purpose in life.

Self-actualization meditation is recommended for:

Awakening dormant talents and potential, carving out our true identity, discovering our purpose in life.

The Twelve Elixirs

TECHNIQUE:

1. Connect the Sun fingers and join the Saturn fingers at the top joint.

2. Close the Jupiter fingers and the thumbs, and join them together.

4. How Do I Materialize?

3. Connect the Mercury fingers at their tips.

Notes

1. Jean Varenne, *Yoga and the Hindu Tradition* (Chicago and London: The University of Chicago Press, 1976), p. 18.

2. Georg Feuerstein, Ph.D., *The Yoga Tradition: It's History, Literature, Philosophy and Practice* (Prescott, Arizona: Hohm Press, 1998), p. 225.

3. Huston Smith, *The World's Religions: A Completely Revised and Updated Edition of The Religions of Man* (New York: Harper San Francisco, A Division of Harper Collins Publishers, 1991), pp. 196-220.

4. Christian De Duve, *Vital Dust: The Origin and Evolution of Life on Earth* (New York: Basic Books, A Subsidiary of Perseus Books, L.L.C.,1995), pp. 1-11.

5. Ibid., pp. 46-82.

6. David Bohm, *Wholeness and the Implicate Order* (London and New York: Routledge, 1995), p. 212.

7. Gordon Fraser; Egil Lillestol; Inge Sellevag, *Introduction by Stephen Hawking. The Search for Infinity: Solving the mysteries of the Universe* (New York: Facts On File, Inc., 1995), pp. 104-105.

8. Paul Davies, *The 5th Miracle: The Search for the Origin and Meaning of Life* (New York, London, Sydney, Singapore: A Touchstone Book, Published by Simon & Schuster, 2000), p. 61.

9. Fred Adams; Greg Laughlin, *The Five Ages of the Universe: Inside the Physics of Eternity* (New York: The Free Press, A Division of Simon & Schuster Inc., 1999), pp. 20-28.

10. Dr. Arne A. Wyller, *The Creating Consciousness: Science as the Language of God* (Denver, Colorado: Divina, a division of MacMurray & Beck, 1999), p. 26.

11. Fritjof Capra, *The Tao of Physics* (Boston: Shambala, 1991), p.73.

12. Ibid., p. 66.

13. Fred Unterseher; Jeannene Hansen; Bob Schlesinger, *Holography Handbook: Making Holograms the Easy Way* (Berkley, California: Ross Books, 1982), pp. 308-332.

14. Steven Pinker, *How the Mind Works* (New York, London: W.W. Norton & Company, 1997), pp. 218-227.

15. Michael Talbot, *The Holographic Universe* (New York: Harper Perennial, A Division of Harper Collins Publishers, 1992), p. 20.

16. Ibid., p. 55.

17. Gordon Fraser; Egil Lillestol; Inge Sellevag, *Introduction by Stephen Hawking. The Search for Infinity: Solving the mysteries of the Universe* (New York: Facts On File, Inc., 1995), pp. 34-35

18. Ibid., pp. 36-37.

19. Fred Unterseher; Jeannene Hansen; Bob Schlesinger, *Holography Handbook: Making Holograms the Easy Way* (Berkley, California: Ross Books, 1982), pp. 310-313.

20. Richard Maurice Bucke, M.D., *Cosmic Consciousness: A Study in the Evolution of the Human Mind* (New York: A Citadel Press Book, Published by Carol Publishing Group,1993), pp. 28-33.

21. Charles Eliot, *Japanese Buddhism* (New York: Barnes & Noble, 1969), pp. 109-110.

22. David Bohm, *Wholeness and the Implicate Order* (London and New York: Routledge, 1995), pp. 150-157.

23. Lama Anagarika Govinda, *Foundations of Tibetan Mysticism* (York Beach, Maine: Samuel Wiser, Inc, 1969), p. 101.

24. Georg Feuerstein, Ph.D., *The Yoga Tradition: It's History, Literature, Philosophy and Practice* (Prescott, Arizona: Hohm Press, 1998), p. 479.

25. Madhu Khanna, *Yantra: The Tantric Symbol of Cosmic Unity* (New York: Thames and Hudson Inc., 1997), pp. 9-29.

26. Ibid., pp. 70-77.

27) Alan Holden, *The Nature of Solids* (New York: Dover Publications, Inc., 1992), p. 50.

28) Fredric Schiffer, M.D., *Of Two Minds: The Revolutionary Science of Dual-Brain Psychology* (New

York: The Free Press, A Division of Simon & Schuster Inc., 1998), p. 5.

29) Ibid., pp.17-45.

30. Madhu Khanna, *Yantra: The Tantric Symbol of Cosmic Unity* (New York: Thames and Hudson Inc., 1997), p. 9.

Bibliography

Adams, Fred; Laughlin, Greg. *The Five Ages of the Universe: Inside the Physics of Eternity.* New York: The Free Press, A Division of Simon & Schuster Inc., 1999.

Arguelles, Jose and Miriam. *Mandala.* Boston and London: Shambhala, 1995.

Bohm, David. *Wholeness and the Implicate Order.* London and New York: Routledge, 1995.

Bucke, Richard Maurice, M.D. *Cosmic Consciousness: A Study in the Evolution of the Human Mind.* New York: A Citadel Press Book, Published by Carol Publishing Group, 1993.

Capra, Fritjof. *The Tao of Physics. Third Edition, Updated.* Boston: Shambala, 1991.

Cole, K.C. *First You Build a Cloud: And Other Reflections on Physics as a Way of Life.* San Diego, New York, London: Harcourt Brace & Company, 1999.

Davies, Paul. *God & The New Physics.* New York: A Touchstone Book, Published by Simon & Schuster, 1984.

_____. *The 5th Miracle: The Search for the Origin and Meaning of Life.* New York, London, Sydney, Singapore: A Touchstone Book, Published by Simon & Schuster, 2000.

Duve, Christian De. *Vital Dust: The Origin and Evolution of Life on Earth.* New York: Basic Books, A Subsidiary of Perseus Books, L.L.C., 1995.

Eliot, Charles. *Japanese Buddhism.* New York: Barnes & Noble, 1969.

Feuerstein, Georg, Ph.D. Foreword by Ken Wilber. *The Yoga Tradition: It's History, Literature, Philosophy and Practice.* Prescott, Arizona: Hohm Press, 1998.

_____. *Tantra: The Path of Ecstasy.* Boston & London: Shambhala, 1997.

Feuerstein, Georg, Ph.D.; and Miller, Jeanine. *The Essence of Yoga: Essays on the Development of Yogic Philosophy from the Vedas to Modern Times.* Rochester, Vermont: Inner Traditions International, 1998.

Fontana, Dr. David. *The Meditator's Handbook: A Comprehensive Guide to Eastern & Western Meditation Techniques.* Boston, MA: Element, 1998.

Fraser, Gordon; Lillestol, Egil; Sellevag, Inge. Introduction by Stephen Hawking. *The Search for Infinity: Solving the mysteries of the Universe.* New York: Facts On File, Inc., 1995.

Govinda, Lama Anagarika. *Foundations of Tibetan Mysticism.* York Beach, Maine: Samuel Wiser, Inc., 1969.

Greene, Brian. *The Elegant Universe: Superstrings, Hidden Dimensions, and the Quest for the Ultimate Theory.* New York: Vintage Books, A Division of Random House, Inc., 2000.

Grof, Stanislav, M.D.; Bennett, Hal Zina, Ph.D. *The Holotropic Mind: The Three Levels of Human Consciousness and How They Shape Our Lives.* Harper San Francisco, A Division of Harper Collins Publishers, 1993.

Hawking, Stephen. *A Brief History of Time. The Updated and Expanded Tenth Anniversary Edition.* New York: Bantam Books, 1998.

H.H. The Dalai Lama. *Ethics For The New Millennium.* New York: Riverhead Books, A Member of Penguin Putnam Inc., 1999.

————. *A Simple Path. Basic Buddhist Teachings by His Holiness The Dalai Lama.* London: Thorsons, An Imprint of Harper Collins Publishers, 2000.

H.H. The Dalai Lama, Tsong-ka-pa & Hopkins, Jeffrey. *Deity Yoga: In Action and Performance Tantra.* Ithaca, New York: Snow Lion Publications, 1987.

Holden, Alan. *The Nature of Solids.* New York: Dover Publications, Inc., 1992.

Jung, Carl G. *Man and his Symbols.* New York: Anchor Books, Doubleday, 1964.

Khanna, Madhu. *Yantra: The Tantric Symbol of Cosmic Unity.* New York: Thames and Hudson Inc., 1997.

Lawlor, Robert. *Sacred Geometry: Philosophy and Practice.* New York: Thames and Hudson Inc., 1998.

Levenson, Claude B. *Symbols of Tibetan Buddhism.* Paris, France: Editions Assouline, 1996.

Maharishi Mahesh Yogi. *Science of Being and Art of Living: Transcendental Meditation.* New York: Meridian, 1963.

————. *TM: Transcendental Meditation.* New York: Donald I. Fine, Inc., 1994.

McDonald, Kathleen. *How To Meditate: A Practical Guide.* Somerville, Massachusetts: Wisdom Publications, 1984.

Monaghan, Patricia, and Viereck, Eleanor G. *Meditation: The Complete Guide.* Novato, California: New World Library, 1999.

Neumann, Erich. *The Origins and History of Consciousness.* Princeton, N.J.: Princeton University Press, 1995.

Park, David. *The Fire Within The Eye: A Historical Essay On The Nature And Meaning of Light.* Princeton, New Jersey: Princeton University Press, 1999.

Pinker, Steven. *How the Mind Works.* New York, London: W.W. Norton & Company, 1997.

Pribram, Karl. *Languages of the Brain.* Monterey, California: Wadsworth Publishing, 1997.

Reed, Henry, Ph.D. *Awakening Your Psychic Powers.* New York: St. Martin's Paperbacks, 1996.

Ronchi, Vasco. *Optics: The Science of Vision.* New York: Dover Publications, Inc., 1991.

Saunders, E. Dale. *Mudra: A Study of Symbolic Gestures in Japanese Buddhist Sculpture.* Princeton, New Jersey: Bollingen Series LVIII, Princeton University Press, 1985.

Schiffer, Fredric, M.D. *Of Two Minds: The Revolutionary Science of Dual-Brain Psychology.* New York: The Free Press, A Division of Simon &Schuster Inc., 1998.

Schimmel, Annemarie. *The Mystery of Numbers.* New York, Oxford: Oxford University Press, 1993.

Smith, Huston. *The World's Religions: A Completely Revised and Updated Edition of The Religions of Man.* New York: Harper San Francisco, A Division of Harper Collins Publishers, 1991.

Talbot, Michael. *The Holographic Universe.* New York: Harper Perennial, A Division of Harper Collins Publishers, 1992.

—————. *Mysticism and the New Physics.* London: Arkana, Penguin Books, 1993.

Tattersall, Ian. *Becoming Human: Evolution & Human Uniqueness.* New York, San Diego, London: Harcourt Brace & Company, 1998.

Unterseher, Fred; Hansen, Jeannene; Schlesinger, Bob. *Holography Handbook: Making Holograms the Easy Way.* Berkley, California: Ross Books, 1982.

Varenne, Jean. *Yoga And the Hindu Tradition.* Chicago and London: The University of Chicago Press, 1976.

Walker, Evan Harris. *The Physics of Consciousness: The Quantum Mind and the Meaning of Life.* Cambridge, Massachusetts: Perseus Books, 1999.

Wolf, Fred Alan. *Taking the Quantum Leap: The New Physics For Non-Scientists.* New York: Harper & Row, 1989.

Wolf, Fred Alan, Ph.D. *The Spiritual Universe: One Physicist's Vision of Spirit, Soul, Matter, and Self.* Portsmouth, NH: Moment Point Press, Inc., 1999.

_____. *The Dreaming Universe: A Mind-Expanding Journey Into The Realm Where Psyche & Physics Meet.* New York: A Touchstone Book, Published by Simon & Schuster, 1994.

Wyller, Dr. Arne A. *The Creating Consciousness: Science as the Language of God.* Denver, Colorado: Divina, A Division of MacMurray & Beck, 1999.

Zohar, Danah. *The Quantum Self: Human Nature and Consciousness Defined By The New Physics.* New York: Quill/William Morrow, 1990.

Zohar, Fanah; Marshall, Ian. *The Quantum Society: Mind, Physics, and a New Social Vision.* New York: Quill, William Morrow, 1994.

Zukav, Gary. *The Dancing Wu Li Masters: An Overview of the New Physics.* New York: Bantam Books, 1980.

Jasmin Akash M.A. - The Creator of Holographic Mudra Meditation

www.ingramcontent.com/pod-product-compliance
Lightning Source LLC
Chambersburg PA
CBHW060807010526
44115CB00003B/14